Principles of
Magick

PRINCIPLES OF MAGICK

A traditionally trained shaman's teachings on the mystic arts

JEFFREY PIERCE

For information regarding permission, write to:

Sage & Scribe, LLC

4742 Liberty Road S, #396

Salem, OR 97302.

ISBN-13: 978-0615785547

ISBN-10: 0615785549

www.sageandscribe.com

Printed in the U.S.A.

Contents

INTRODUCTION

We are taught that mystical spirituality is the dominion of a few select individuals who have a unique connection through which to dispense wisdom and knowledge, to acquire and teach magickal arts, and through which they and only they can truly hear the voices of the gods.

Thankfully, nothing could be further from the truth.

We're also taught that we need to master phrases and gestures in order to wield mystical energies. Well-meaning teachers have passed on lessons from their well-meaning teachers, insisting that there is one way to work magick. That through meditation, fasting and prayer we can reach levels of reality that we would be unable to unlock through any other method. We find ourselves believing that the secrets exist in ancient arcane texts, in traditions passed down through the generations and hidden away from the eyes of men. By devoting ourselves to teachers, through a path wrought with dedication, sacrifice and perseverance, we believe that we can prove ourselves worthy to receive a gift from the gods and finally embrace the power or peace or love that we seek.

The process is infinitely easier than all of that.

The big secret is that you already have access to all of the things that you seek. You are extraordinarily powerful, infinitely wise, and tremendously adept. There is absolutely nothing that you cannot do, no height that you cannot reach, no secret whose answer is not already at your fingertips. We are spiritual beings, an expression of the Divine with all of the power of a god or goddess inherently in our possession. The problem, in its entirety, is that we've chosen to experience reality from a mundane and physical perspective. In order to do that, we agreed to accept a certain amount of lies as truth; we've chosen to believe in an illusion rather than the reality it hides.

What we have to realize is that the journey before us isn't one where we reach for some unattainable goal, forever tempering our spirit in a mystical fire, honing skills to reach ever higher levels of reality. The journey is a simple process of discovering why we have chosen to live this lifetime and removing the illusions that prevent us from doing just that. The more illusions we remove, the more truth we see. The more truth that's available to us, the more power we wield. The secret is that this is not a process of gathering insight and wisdom, but simply letting go of the things we have chosen to separate us from who we truly are - powerful, spiritual beings who have agreed to experience reality from a physical perspective.

There's a simple spiritual law that I was taught by one of my teachers. "To uncover the truth, you must dig deep below the layer upon which you currently stand. Digging deep is simply a matter of removing that which stands between you and what you seek to reach. Each layer is an illusion, filled with attachments, fears, and desires. The more that you remove, the freer you will become; the more you remove, the closer you will be to the truth."

If we focus this law on the very nature of our existence, it would encourage us to rewind time as we perceive it. We cannot look at our lives as adults and understand the source we emanated from. Our only choice is to remove that which stands between us and our goal - the understanding of who we are in the bigger perspective of reality, a perspective framed by the knowledge of our origin.

At first glance, we would assume that we would find the answers in our first breath, in the moment when we initially entered this lifetime. After all, from our current perspective it's at that point that we were closest to the spirit world, unburdened by the memories, prejudices, and fears we have gathered over the decades. So we remove our career, our family, our personal history that has woven the story of who we have become. In doing so, we strip away the years until we're once more an infant. But even in a newly born state, we are simply a mortal child in a sea of mortal children. That's only one level of who we are. It's not the core of our existence. There was something before, something that created the first spark of life in our mother's womb, a place where even that spark originated. Where did we come from? What process led to the emergence of our soul in the identity we now wear as a physical form?

Employing our first tool in our spiritual journey, we realize that if the answer is that we are but one of many mortals born into this life, then we haven't reached the source of our truth. We can still dig deeper. To do so, we must remove what stands between us and our goal. We must go to a level that existed before we were a child, before we began to build the identity we hold in our current incarnation. So we go back farther, rewinding time until we peer into the generations before our birth. We see ancestors stretching back to the beginning of recorded time, the spark of our existence being kindled in an era reflected not so much by history as it is by scientific theory and theology. Even at this point in our understanding of who we are, our identity is obscured by the countless people existing all over our planet. Another level beckons to be removed and we realize that we must dig even deeper.

We go back first to the beginning of mankind and then, back even before the beginning of the human race. We begin to see ourselves, not as a single member of a single species, but as one thread in an infinite tapestry of life that began on a small blue-green planet that will eventually be called Earth. As we begin to embrace this perspective, we gain the understanding that our planet is but one of many planets in our solar system, and our solar system is one of many solar systems in our galaxy. Another level to be removed. We need to dig deeper still.

In this manner we rewind existence to the time before our solar system was formed, before our galaxy emerged into the weave of reality, even before our universe was born. We dig ever deeper until we reach a moment where there is nothing in all of existence but a single divine energy. There is no time, no matter, nothing but the energy from which all existence will be created. Call it God, Spirit, the Goddess, the Divine - call it what you will, but at last we have reached the level where there is nothing more to be removed, where we find out who we truly are.

And we are Divine.

It is not from a box of odds and ends that the universe will be created. It isn't from a pile of cosmic dust or a handful of amino acids that our planet and the life it contains will be formed. At this point in the game, none of that exists. The only thing that can be found in all of existence is the infinite, timeless energy we understand as God.

One of the great secrets of this reality is that not only are we never separated from this source, not only are we created from this source, but that we are this source. All of existence is. For all intents and purposes, we are God. Not just us, but every living thing on this planet, even the stones, the wind, and the planet itself.

The key is that this is a pretty big concept for any of us to comprehend. So we consciously limit what God can be. We place the Divine in comfortable little boxes that say, "God is this, but not that." We like the idea that there is a cosmic Big Brother or Big Sister out there, watching over us and taking care of us, that life and all of its infinite varieties of expression aren't our responsibility, but that they belong in the hands of Someone Else.

Ironically, that's a completely valid perspective - even if it's ultimately flawed. In order to perceive reality from a physical perspective, we've had to accept the illusion that there are certain limitations to our existence. One of these is that we're separated from God, that we aren't divine but through our own flaws - whether it's the Christian concept of sin, a shaman's quest to return to a state of balance and oneness with the divine, or a magickal practitioner's belief that they can only reach the source of sacred power through study and the mastery of certain skills - there is something that stands between us and God, that cuts us off from the Divine and makes us something less than sacred. This illusion provides us with the framework to live life as a unique expression of the Divine with a limited perspective and unique experience that is as individual as we are as human beings. If the Divine is truly all-encompassing, then it must exist in every expression of reality. As counter-intuitive as it may seem, for the Divine to embrace every life, every moment of reality, it must also manifest as an expression of life that sees itself as being separate from the sacred, living a flawed, limited, finite lifetime.

That limited perspective would be us.

As human beings there are two critical stages to our physical existence, an existence that, for most of us, will span multiple incarnations or lifetimes. The first stage is learning to find our reason for existing and by honoring that reason, actively engaging in a process of learning to live a life where we are at peace and filled with love - and typically manifest a great deal of joy. The second stage is deciding to reach beyond that first stage and consciously begin the process of spiritual evolution, a cycle of growth that will enable us to reclaim the perspective that we are divine and leave the need to incarnate into this physical realm behind us.

Gaining that perspective isn't a process of gathering new insight, but letting go of old illusions. In doing so, we gain the understanding of our own divinity. Think about that for just a moment. If we are truly divine but have convinced ourselves that we are not, then we have chosen to limit our own power. If we truly are divine, with all that it infers, what happens when we not only begin to understand that perspective, but begin to believe and live it?

Much of Western occultism focuses on creating states of existence (usually through ritual and ceremony) where we transition beyond the mundane to interact with the spiritual. In that space, the practitioner, shaman, or adept interacts with spiritual energies in order to bend them to their will. The path that I was taught moves the person, not the sacred space, away from the mundane and into the spiritual. Eventually a place is reached where ceremony, tools, ritual implements and techniques are completely unnecessary to achieve a level that was challenging (at best) to reach without them. Magick, for lack of a better definition, becomes an extension of the person's daily life, rather than something they seek through ceremonial means.

One of my teachers explained the concept like this: "There's a shamanic tradition that uses hallucinogenic herbs to reach a certain shamanic state. What most people don't realize is that the herbs are only a crutch, that the shaman is expected to learn to reach that state alone, without the assistance of the herb. The first time they journey, the new shaman will be given a full dose of the herb in order to see the place that they are intended to reach. With each subsequent journey, the dose will be lessened and the shaman will have to develop and rely on their own abilities to reach that state of consciousness. Eventually, the shaman can reach the same level without the herb and use of the herb at that point would actually limit their own abilities."

If we look at our meditations, our ceremonies, our incantations and ritual elements as what they are - tools - then it's a simple step to understand that they should fall away as we develop our own abilities. The training wheels eventually came off our bicycles when we learned to ride, just as we eventually left our water wings at the side of the swimming pool. The tradition in which I was taught follows the same template, but the concept can be extended to any spiritual practice as well as a wide range of physical endeavors.

It's important to realize that the illusions that we've chosen to use to limit our perspective aren't like a pair of glasses that can simply be lifted off of our eyes and set aside. Imagine that your body is encased in a sheath of opaque threads like a mummy's wrappings. While the threads can be seen through when present in small numbers, en masse they are capable of blocking out all light. The threads must be cut away strand-by-strand. Occasionally we'll make breakthroughs in our path that will enable us to cut through several threads at a time, but each must be systematically removed, just as they were systematically put in place. As we begin to lose our illusions, effectively cutting the threads, two things will begin to happen. First of all, we'll begin to see life and reality with more clarity. Light will begin to seep through the shroud we wear. Second, as the threads begin to fall away, we'll rediscover the movement we possess as spiritual beings, this movement manifesting as a wide range of abilities such as spiritual dreaming, precognition, shamanic journeying and the like.

There is nothing otherworldly or fantastic about any of this. It's our birthright as the spiritual beings we truly are.

As we begin to move through this guide together, it is important that I give you one more piece to carry with you throughout this journey.

I tell all of my students, "Your heart is your map and your intuition your compass. Follow them. They will not lead you astray." This may be the most important guideline in all of magick, even more important than the foundational concept of, "As below, so above." That sense that something "feels right" or "feels wrong" is your intuition. It will always point in the direction that you need to go, even if you don't always understand the reasons why you are being led in that direction.

People downplay our feelings, our emotions, and our heart all the time. It could easily be argued that your heart is the connecting point between your incarnated identity and the subtle realms - magick, the spirit world, and your own spirit or soul. If you shut down your heart, if you push it aside, if you ignore the validity and power of your own feelings, your ability to work magick will also slowly fade away. As your heart reemerges from exile, your ability to work magick will improve. It's a rather simple equation.

To write a book like "Principles of Magick," I first had to follow my own heart and intuition through the pages. It was necessary for me to write from the core of my own path, rather than to attempt to water it down into generalities that spoke to the intricacies of all of our perspectives. There are countless ways to approach magick. The deities you look to - whether you choose to follow an ancient pagan deity or the Christian Jesus - are utterly irrelevant. Magick isn't tied to a particular system of belief, nor does it reflect a particular aspect of the Divine. It is simply a tool that each of us has access to; it is a path that leads us deeper into the mystical nature of reality.

Among the many paths that I have walked, I've reached a place in my life where I simply identify myself as pagan - with a little "p." It's not a proper noun or a formalized religion such as Paganism or being Neo-Pagan. As a traditionally trained shaman, I learned to walk between the worlds; in my own practice as a spiritual teacher, I've learned to walk between the paths of my students.

That said, throughout this guide you will find concepts that may seem strange to you. I speak of the Goddess and the God, not because I worship them, but because they are extremely useful tools for dividing spiritual reality into themes that I can understand. You'll see that I reference scripture at one point because it accurately reflects a principle that is integral to magick. None of that is intended to proselytize, an attempt that would seem somewhat silly as I personally identify with a very informal, personal approach to spirituality.

However, if you can set your prejudices and preconceived ideas aside and look beyond the labels to the illustrations each concept holds, you'll find aspects of your own life and your own path. Magick isn't the property of any one religion. It is a tool and a path that leads us from a limited way of perceiving and interacting with our world to a perspective that isn't nearly as constrained. Magick can be found in a desperate plea, a congregations' prayer, a lover's intimate embrace, honest compassion or gratitude, through a child's eyes, in a coven's chant, or painted across the sky in a breathtaking sunset. The secret is that each of those moments - moments that resonate with our heart and our intuition - also lead to something deeper if we allow them to do so.

This book simply outlines that journey from the perspective of one seeker. May you be as blessed by these words as I have been by each and every student who has come my way.

CHAPTER ONE

A PLACE TO START

On March 21, 1987 I made a pact with the Divine. I didn't want someone else's interpretation of God. I didn't want to see Spirit through the filter of a religion created by man. I wanted to experience all of it, firsthand, for myself. In exchange, I was willing to go wherever I was led, walk through any door that was opened for me, and embrace any path that I was led to explore.

Looking back on that day, I never would have guessed where the journey would take me.

From Christianity I learned of passion and emotion from the Pentecostals and of miracles, love, servitude, and balance, not just from the successes of Jesus as portrayed by a disciple of the Apostle Peter, but from his failures as well. Trained as a traditional shaman, I explored inner landscapes and the spirit world, learning the role of ego and sacrifice, discovering how everything is filled with Spirit, power, and love. Taoism taught me of the nature of the Divine and how to release my preconceived ideas and continually expand my awareness. Wicca and witchcraft taught me about spellwork and ceremony, of the balance between light and dark, and how everything is a cycle, continually turning and spiraling on its own beautiful way. From Tantra, I learned acceptance and love, how each thing we like or dislike is simply a mirror of ourselves. Buddhism taught me of compassion, of stilling the mind and releasing one's attachments. In Asatru, I discovered the importance of honor, honesty, and strength, of living in the moment, not for the moment, and that the story one leaves behind is of more value than the wealth one accrues. Other teachers along the way imparted their own lessons and wisdom to me, and I gratefully and humbly learned from each opportunity that I was presented.

There were so many systems of belief, so many spiritual paths with so much valid wisdom and insight to share.

So which path is right?

After all, if there's a single correct path to follow, any exploration of magick that leads one down an alternate road will, by definition, reach a dead end. I wasn't interested in fancy titles or certificates from mystery schools. What I wanted was to experience the Divine, the sacred "All is One" behind Creation. Such a path would hold real power, not simply illusions and empty promises. What's more is that for the magick to be real, it would have to work. If I couldn't successfully achieve a desired outcome through a mystical technique, then that technique was only a marker on a map, not the destination itself, and if didn't work, it was most likely a marker that indicated I'd veered off course.

What I discovered is that there isn't a right path. There are those paths that teach us what we need, that provide us with the insight, wisdom, philosophy and techniques to take the next step in our spiritual journey, but that's all that any path is capable of doing. Tragically, it seems as if there is a predisposition for the leaders of any school of spiritual thought to find a piece of the Truth and then stop growing and evolving, holding on to that fragment of the whole tightly and claiming that the piece they hold is entire Truth, because it is Truth and it is real.

And that was an unexpected lesson that each path taught me - that each system of belief is a path, not a destination. Once it becomes a destination, once a spiritual path holds on to the Truth instead of seeking to delve deeper, to learn more, to give that Truth away freely, then it falls in love with itself. It stares too long in the mirror, complimenting itself on its good looks, on its importance, and even worse, eventually losing sight of the piece of the Truth it once held and replacing it with its demands to be worshiped.

What we as spiritual seekers must remember is that no system of belief holds all of the answers or the complete fullness of Truth. Each spiritual school is a lesson - it is not the final answer. To make matters worse, we're so desperate for love, so desperate for Truth, that when we find the smallest piece of either, we accept it blindly. "This is Love," we're told. "This is the whole Truth." We can see for ourselves that it's real love, that it's real truth; it's just not the entire picture. But it's real - so we hold on to it tightly, defending it against anyone who would challenge its validity, who would question whether there might be more to the bigger picture.

I do not have the whole of the Truth. I do not fully love. Each day, I embrace the validity of my limitations and seek to embrace a little more of the bigger picture, to understand a little more of the Truth, to unconditionally and fully love a little bit more. Rather than embracing a particular path, I've tried to understand how we grow and the parts of our being that come into play as we learn, as we discover, as we grow.

As I have come to understand the mechanism behind our spiritual growth, there are three key Paths to follow when deepening your spiritual practice. All three of these Paths hold secrets of the greater Truth, secrets that open doors that lead deeper into the realm of magick and spiritual mysteries. Each of these avenues to spirituality represents a key piece of the greater puzzle and all three of these weave together to create a cohesive whole.

It's not uncommon for us to embrace a single Path for a time, only to completely abandon it when it is time for us to focus on the next portion of our spiritual practice. Approaching these Paths one at a time provides us with strong individual threads to weave into the cord of our greater spiritual path. Likewise, it is completely appropriate for us to dabble in each Path simultaneously. Doing so provides us with understanding, wisdom, and perspective from the very beginning of our spiritual journey.

TH OF LOVE

When we hear the word "love," one of two thoughts generally appear in our minds. The first is romantic love. "Oh, I love him!" It's a love of Valentine's Day cards and first kisses and living happily ever after. The second is that of pleasure. We love peanut butter and jelly or a good steak or fine chocolate. We make love. "Don't you just love these new shoes?"

Yet both visions of love, at best, are a poor reflection of only the tiniest fraction of Love.

Love is power, plain and simple. It is the wild card that trumps any challenge, any lesson, any situation. You can't defeat, beat, or overcome Love. If a situation unfolds one way, Love saves the day. If a situation unfolds the other way, Love willingly sacrifices itself. If it plays out a third way, Love makes even the good times better. You can't overcome it. You can't suppress it. You cannot defeat Love.

It's probably one of the greatest mysteries in modern spirituality, how much we talk about love but how little we practice it. The Path of Love is challenging for the mind to grasp because real, full, unconditional Love is, at first glance, a paradox. Love is power and sacrifice. It is both life and death. Love is active and passive, it is strong yet gentle, it can heal and it can destroy.

When we think of love, we think of an emotion or feeling. Some of us may even think of a vibration, although we've been taught to say that and most of us don't really understand what being a vibration entails.

Love? Love is a key.

If you think of any moment in time and begin categorizing all of the pieces that compose that moment, you'll come up with quite a list. There are the people involved, the emotional and mental state of each, where the energy is flowing, the energy that is being held in reserve (things unsaid, a desire to see what happens before you act), the environment, the history of the people in the situation, endless levels of symbolism and the power that those symbols hold - the list goes on and on.

If you could take all of the bits and pieces from that moment and capture it with a single word, understanding that word would give you an idea of what it is to see energetic reality. Now, using that as a framework for understanding the concept, imagine the energetic reality of fully unconditional Love.

Love is the only energy that consistently transforms what it touches. What is hidden away is brought forth. What is hurt, heals. What is strong is made stronger. The challenge for us when we find ourselves on The Path of Love is that we first have to apply those lessons to ourselves. We have to allow our hidden parts to be brought forth, our hurts to be healed, and our strengths to be made even stronger. That's a vulnerable, challenging process for many of us - but it nurtures the love, compassion, understanding, patience, acceptance, and gentleness in us that is key to fully and unconditionally loving others. It allows our own ego to die while bringing our own heart to life.

THE PATH OF MIND

The Path of Mind is most simply understood if we think of Mind, not as an expression of deductive reasoning and analysis, but as a filter formed of preconceived ideas and prejudices that changes what we experience. Our Mind is filled to the brim with energetic structures that I refer to as filters. These filters act much like a colored gel placed over a light. Instead of the light shining through in all of its wavelengths, it is reduced to certain colors, limited by the gel (or filter) that we've put into place.

Embracing The Path of Mind is as much a process of removing ways of thinking as it is of embracing new thoughts and concepts. The two approaches are simply flip sides of the same coin. To embrace a new thought requires that new filters are put into place. To change a preconceived idea requires that the existing filters be removed. It's like swapping out an indigo colored gel for midnight blue, then deep blue, then primary blue, then eggshell, then baby blue, then off white, then smoky glass, then clear. It isn't a misstep to put new filters in place; they actually act as stepping stones on our journey to clearly see the landscape before us. The key is to admit to ourselves that we don't see the entire picture, even if we're not aware of the overlooked pieces. Eventually this process leads to a point where you begin to release the need to attach a predefined label to anything and you simply live in the moment. At its ultimate expression, The Path of the Mind exists with simple awareness of the current moment and does not judge anything as good or evil but simply recognizes it as part of (or a reflection of) the whole.

Taoism has always represented the ultimate expression of Mind to me, simply because of that path's concept of the Tao. I like to think of the Tao as another name for God. What is the Tao? If you can name it, it's not the Tao. The Tao is simply too "fill in the blank" to be limited by a word, idea, or phrase. If you replace "the Tao" with "God/Goddess/Spirit/Universe" and begin to describe how you see the Divine - the whole concept, not just its individual aspects - you start to understand the role of filters and how they alter our perception.

"Well, I see Goddess as an expression of feminine energy."

Then by the very concept of using the Tao as a mirror of Goddess, Goddess must be more than feminine energy because feminine energy can be named. To name something is to define it. To define something is to limit it. If Goddess is truly the full embodiment of the Divine, then Goddess can have no limitations.

"Okay, so I see Goddess as an expression of both feminine and masculine energy."

Once again, you've named something by using gender roles. By naming it, you've limited it.

"Alright... So Goddess is simply a reflection of everything that is."

Two problems here: One is that if something is a reflection it's not the source (and vice versa) and if it's everything that is, it's not everything that was or will one day be... Or may never be.

If we look at this concept as if some game show host is constantly pushing a buzzer and announcing in a mocking tone, "Wrong! Try again," the whole journey becomes frustrating and counterproductive. However, if we approach it from a perspective of, "If Goddess is more than what I realized, what more can She be?" we begin to gain a greater understanding of the Divine rather than simply losing pieces that we once passionately held close to our hearts.

This same process can be directed at every concept in our lives and paths - from our diet to our magickal practices to our calling to our interpersonal conflicts to why we like ice cream. As you can see, each step through this process illuminates more and more where our preconceived ideas (or filters) can be found. By asking ourselves, "Why do I feel this way? What about the Goddess being feminine appeals to me?" we begin to discover the underlying reasons that gave birth to these filters. Each investigative question we ask ourselves illuminates more of our inner landscape. When we see ourselves more clearly, by extension, we begin to see everything more clearly. By working through the underlying reasons behind our filters, by addressing the wounds, fears, or needs that empower those filters, we find that the filters themselves are no longer useful to us and they simply fall away on their own. And while this has obvious appeal as a tool that can see through the challenges before us, imagine what happens when you begin to prepare for a rite or a magickal working and you can see all of the ritual elements, from your intent to the symbolism of your rite, with such clarity.

Eastern philosophy is rich with these sorts of thoughts, approaches, and exercises, reflecting The Path of the Mind. And while it may be cliché, how many times, watching a movie or reading a book, have you heard a master tell their student, "First you must master your own thoughts."

That, in a nutshell, is The Path of the Mind.

THE PATH OF SPIRIT

In magick, whether it's worked by a shaman, turned by a witch, cast by a Wiccan, or called upon by a spirit-filled Christian, one seeks to move closer to the spirit realm. If you're drawing nearer to the physical realm, you hold on more tightly to the tangible things before you; if you're drawing closer to the spirit realm, you're connecting with

beyond the concrete structure of our world. I've
ght the argument was a simple one: how can you
ly understand something (in this case, the realm
you never experience it firsthand?
rs ago, I slipped into the back of a Pentecostal
Easter service where a relative of mine was performing in
the service. Around me were concepts that any pagan would
be familiar with. Here folks were engaging in ceremonial
spiritual dance. There, members of the congregation were
praising God, surrendering their ego and opening themselves
up to the flow of energy.

Love is our travel guide along this path, giving
us a framework for our spiritual growth. Mind allows us
to consider the thoughts, philosophies, and experiences
we encounter along the way, using them to gain a greater
understanding of the whole and removing the filters that
have limited our perspective to that point on our path. Spirit
is experiential. It's what it's like to feel the Divine, to touch
spiritual energy, to experience a mystical moment firsthand.

It's also the easiest of all of the paths to embrace.

In my opinion, it's one of the reasons why there
has been such a huge upswing in the interest in paganism
and various magickal paths over the last two decades. Our
culture is sadly deficient in Love. Likewise, The Path of Mind
is almost completely absent as we're taught what to believe,
not how to discover and consider our own beliefs.

Magick? Anyone can do magick. You don't need to
be surrounded by Love or taught the concepts behind it.
A candle and a few sincerely whispered words are all you
need to really connect - and if resources are limited, even the
candle is optional.

Experiencing something makes it real. Every path
should understand this. Ask anyone, "How did you feel
when you first embraced your path?" and you are certain
to receive a very heartfelt answer in return. Christians
are actually encouraged to witness and tell you what they
experienced, but any follower of any spiritual path can tell
you about their personal experience with that path. Those
who embrace The Path of Spirit simply want to experience
the mystical for themselves. It isn't that they're narcissistic
or lack faith or even that they want validation that they've

made the right choice. They want to delve into the mysteries of reality, not through books or lectures or cultivating love, but by experiencing it firsthand.

This is tremendously important to keep in mind as the vast majority of magick takes place on The Path of Spirit. Magick isn't a process where we isolate ourselves from the flow of reality and manipulate those threads from a sterile and separate place. Each time we work magick we place ourselves in that working as well. This applies not simply to ritual or spellwork but also to our interpersonal relationships. If it is true that All is One then how we treat those around us is just as important as how we interact with the spirit realm. If it is true that All is One then the intent and manner in which we approach another human being, their energy, their path, the ritual of our relationship, and the sacred ground of the connection between us, meets the definition of magick as surely as any spell pulled from an ancient grimoire. If it is true that All is One then it is equally as important that we approach ourselves with honor, integrity, compassion, and love as it is to engage in the greatest humanitarian pursuit. If it is true that All is One then not only are we deeply integrated into the magick we work, but everything we do in our lives and on our paths begins with us. We are where both the magick and the change we seek to bring about begins; it is impossible to separate us from our workings or to craft those workings from qualities that we don't exhibit in other areas of our lives.

WHAT ABOUT BODY?

People have asked me, "What about The Path of Body? Isn't there such a thing?" I've heard every argument from sensualists to Tantra practitioners, from athletes to aesthetics.

Body offers perspective; it doesn't offer a Path.

The easiest way to understand this is to think of Body, not as an energetic Path in itself, but as a conduit simultaneously keeping us connected to physical reality while allowing us to experience the energies of Love, Mind, and Spirit in all of their forms and combinations. If Love, Mind, and Spirit were our power sources, Body would be the wires connecting those sources and carrying the energy (or more accurately, allowing us to perceive it).

There are things we can do with Body that improve our ability to experience the other Paths. When I was studying shamanism, I was required to restrict the types of food that I ate up to three days before a rite and to fast the day of the ritual. During my time exploring Buddhism, I was a devout vegetarian. In just a general sense, I find that my ability to experience energy of any type is much more acute when I'm physically fit, drinking plenty of water, and getting enough sleep.

Sex, at its best, is a blending of Love and Spirit connected through the conduit of Body. Martial arts are typically a blending of Mind and Spirit unified through Body. The list of combinations is almost endless. Body isn't a Path in itself, but it can enhance the experience of almost any path for us.

THE RIGHT WAY FOR ME

There is no right way to approach any of these Paths. Embrace them one at a time, embrace bits and pieces of them all at once, it's completely up to you. You can spend a lifetime exploring one Path or a lifetime bouncing back and forth between several. You can devote your life to a conduit – for instance, martial arts – and learn of both Mind and Spirit as they unify through your Body.

It's unimportant which Path you embrace or the order that you embrace them in. It's even unimportant that you consciously embrace any Path. What's useful is simply being aware of their existence.

And while that may seem like an odd approach to take, it's unbelievably useful.

You are unique, an original blessing, incomparable and unlike any other. There is no one approach that works for you. There's no one approach that works for any of us. We learn to navigate through life, using our heart as our map and our intuition as our compass and the journey that we take is as unique as we are as individuals.

It isn't important which route you take to spiritual growth and evolution. That choice is entirely up to you. However, it's important to note the pitfalls, the places where people get stuck. No one Path holds the entirety of the Truth. No one Path is the right Path. They're all simply fragmented reflections of the greater whole, resonating with Love, Mind, and Spirit in turn.

Remember this. It's these Paths, not a particular system of belief, that are important. These Paths are reflections of yourself, of the avenues within you that lead you closer to the Divine. If you begin to search for the Love, Mind, or Spirit within a system of belief, that system's pieces of Truth will be made known to you. The journey takes us from place to place, learning and growing at each stop along the way. By knowing what to look for, you'll have a better understanding of what to hold on to, what to discard, and when it's time for you to move to the next stop along your path.

WHY IS ANY OF THAT IMPORTANT?

I have a feeling that my students occasionally grow frustrated with my responses to some of their questions. When they approach me with a question that essentially asks, "I'm almost there, but I'm stuck. Here's what I've done so far. If you were in my shoes, what would you do next?" then I am always happy to offer suggestions, teach new techniques, and offer supplemental lessons on the spot that paint the landscape for them and offer them options.

It's when they try to rush ahead of where they are on their path that my answers begin to become vague. "What's my calling? In the bigger scheme of things, what does this new piece mean to me? I just discovered my spirit-name/totem-animal/spirit-guide and I'm wondering, now that it has presented itself to me, how it wants me to interact with it more deeply?"

Love, Mind, and Spirit may seem like touchy-feely philosophies, rather than an integral part of a magick path.

Only Spirit seems to have any relevance on the path ahead of us. What's important to remember is that we are seeking to work real magick, with tangible results, and do so in such a way that we transcend the need to rely on physical tools in our practices. To do so, we need to reclaim our birthright as powerful spiritual beings. When seen from a perspective that is willing to be patient and allow the journey before us to evolve and unfold, it makes much more sense to move beyond the grip of our self-imposed illusions and limitations rather than learning to work within them.

Love is power, plain and simple. Mind allows us to release fear and preconceived ideas. Spirit shows us the seams in reality where we can peek between the cracks of the physical realm and see that truly All is One - and then it allows us to experience that for ourselves.

"Great," you think. "But I picked up this book to learn magick. How does any of that help me?"

Imagine that someone has worked some seriously bad mojo against you and one of the "things that go bump in the night" has been placed on your tail. After the initial, "Holy crap! There's a big scary thing after me!" your next thought is, "What do I do about it?"

Someone steeped in modern magick would most likely guard and ward their physical space. Building a boundary of salt, placing a broom across the doorway, scattering iron nails across entryways, and a vast array of other protective magicks would immediately be worked. This is generally seen as a first step, a tactic to buy yourself enough time to work a full banishing.

But what happens when the "night bumper" simply crosses those boundaries and wards as if they never existed?

Allowing your path to unfold and evolve makes it your own; you develop a fluidity that is lacking in the practices of those who have simply learned a paint-by-numbers approach. What's more is that you aren't anchored to tools, or even ritual, which means that you aren't anchored to preconceived notions if you choose to release them.

So a night bumper is set on your trail. Meet it in love. Love is power. The secret is discovering that not only do you are you able to extend love to others, but you are able to also extend love to yourself. You don't need to walk up to the big creepy and say, "Hello there, demon-y thought-form thingy. I just wanted you to know that I love you. Would you like a hug?" You could. It's a valid approach, but you could also step forward and meet it with love *for yourself.*

"You aren't welcome here," you would say. "This is my home and my hearth. Begone. Do not return." Imagine a disinterested stranger dispassionately reading those lines from a script. Now pay attention to the energetic difference as you imagine the person who loves you more than any other stating them as an act of protection and defiance on your behalf.

When those words are said in love - even love for yourself - that approach is infused with power, generally more so than even the most carefully constructed rite. Why? Because love is power. It's the difference between shaving off layers of a magickally infused crystal to make a potion that you'll drink in a rite during which you'll set a boundary, and simply taking the entire crystal in your hands as a mystical weapon, approaching the critter and saying, "No. This is *my* place and *I* will you gone."

Mind? You realize that the night bumper doesn't naturally exist in our realm. If it's difficult for you to cross over into their realm, then it is equally difficult for it to exist here. When I approach things like this from the aspect of Mind [and they've popped up a couple of times; we'll discuss it further in Chapter Sixteen], my approach tends to go something like this:

"Hmmmm... So the structure of reality requires a massive expenditure of energy and focus for this thing to physically interact in this realm. If it comes from a subtle realm, then magick has as much of an influence on it as gravity does on me. Symbolism is the language of magick [don't worry - we'll cover that], which means if I do this," at which point I blow out in one long exhaled breath like I'm trying to put out the candles on a birthday cake, "and I focus on the symbolism of the action, the creature will simply blow away and return to its world." And it does.

So, it may seem that considering things like Love, Mind, and Spirit may be a pretty silly way of working magick, but if you're suddenly in need of a magickal defense, does it make more sense to work an involved rite or simply and literally blow the opposing energy away?

That's the power in allowing your path the room to evolve and unfold. Know yourself, know your path. If you are truly divine, then knowing yourself equates to knowing the Divine. As counterintuitive as it may seem, the more you focus on Love, the more power you gain; the more you focus on Mind, the more clearly that you can see a situation, its strengths and potential as well as its weaknesses and limitations; the more you focus on Spirit, the more clearly you can see how all of the pieces fit together.

Your heart is your map and your intuition is your compass. Follow them. They will not lead you astray. They are the only tools with which you can fully evolve your path and allow it to completely unfold. After all, it's not my path you're building. It's *your* path. You're the expert regarding what is best for you. Even if you don't have all of the answers yet, if you follow your heart and your intuition, you will not only uncover those answers one by one, but you'll gain the wisdom, insight, and perspective to apply them to your own path. Such an approach guarantees that you will always have the potential before you to grow and experience more than you did the day before.

CHAPTER TWO

HOW MAGICK WORKS

If magick is real then it must exist within the established framework of our universe. In order for magick to influence a moment or object that is already governed by measurable laws, then magick must already be integrated into the same system which those measurable laws govern. If the two were separate and exclusive, the established laws would simply cancel each other out.

Think about it this way: when we throw a baseball straight up into the air, a number of factors (velocity, gravity, etc.) combine to dictate when that ball will stop its ascent and begin its return to earth. If you toss the ball with little more than a gentle nudge, it won't go very high; if you hurl it with all your might, chances are it will reach a much greater altitude. If we could measure the strength in our arm and control all of the other variables, we would discover that a specific amount of effort would throw a ball with a standard weight and shape to a specific height.

Various additional factors come into play that will change the flight of the ball, even when we throw it with the same amount of force. For instance, if you're throwing the ball in the midst of a downpour or windstorm, the strong winds and heavy rain will impact the ball's flight; if you attempt to do so in a tornado or hurricane, chances are you're going to achieve results that weren't even hinted at during your test throws. Standing indoors, your ball's ascent will most likely be restricted by the height of the ceiling. While the list of factors isn't endless, each is very real.

When we work magick, our working is framed by natural laws. This isn't limitation, but harmony. To exist as a real part of reality, it is absolutely necessary that magick is seamlessly integrated as one of the laws that dictate the flow of reality. It must work as a synthesis; magick cannot circumvent the structure of the natural world or suspend natural laws. It acts much more like the wind or rain on our thrown ball, working with and limited by other forces (gravity, the weight of the ball, etc.) to change the ball's path. Sometimes our ball will simply return to our hand wet; sometimes the hurricane may carry it away and we'll never know how high the ball went or even where it landed. Regardless of the outcome, the wind and rain work in concert with the other natural laws.

We often approach magick from a perspective of unintended arrogance. Our desire in hand, we work a rite to bring it about, failing to consider the spiritual ecosystems that we will impact if our working goes according to our plan. We wouldn't set off fireworks in a tinderbox of a dry grassland no matter how badly we wanted to see the pyrotechnic light show, yet we seek out our desires without considering how a successful working would impact the rest of reality, other people, and even our own path.

Imagine for a moment that you have a very strong romantic crush on a friend who thinks highly of you but clearly considers you nothing more than a good friend. One day, as you're poking through a used bookstore, you come across an ancient leather-bound tome of love spells. As you flip through the book, you see one that is purported to be able to change a friend's affection into romantic love. Excited that you have a solution to your quandary, you purchase the book, run home, gather the implements that the chosen spell requires, and work the rite.

Now let's imagine that the spell works as advertised. Your friend calls you to let you know that they need to find some time to talk with you. A meeting is arranged. As you sit across from them, they confess their love for you, unsure how they had only seen you as a friend for so long. You reveal that you have felt the same way about them for a very long time. You're happy; they're happy; what could be better?

THE PROBLEM WITH MAGICK

The first problem is that the proposed scenario is completely fictional.

Stretch your arms straight out from the shoulders as if you were imagining that you were an airplane or a bird. That space - a large sphere that extends to just beyond your fingertips and envelops every part of you in an unbroken sphere - is what I refer to as your reality bubble. Your reality bubble isn't an imaginary concept, but a well-tested tool that emerged from working with literally hundreds of students who consistently experienced similar results with the same series of exercises. In a balanced, open individual, that sphere is well-defined; as we are wounded, we tend to pull it in toward our center, but it is always there. While awareness (in all its forms) can expand beyond your sphere, that is a separate phenomena that interacts with and builds off of your reality bubble.

You are in complete and total control of everything that takes place within your reality bubble in every way that is truly lasting and important. Sure, I can ambush you with a surprise hug and be warmly greeting you before you're even aware my arms are around you, but the physical realm is largely inconsequential where reality is concerned. What matters isn't what you're presented with, but how you respond to it. The energy of my hug and your energetic response to it is the fabric of magick; the physical arms around your shoulders are a momentary experience that will have long faded before the energy of the embrace.

I could present you with the warmest, most loving energy possible and you could simply block it out. Doing so isn't simply a matter of rejecting the energetic gesture, but actually subtly realigns numerous energetic processes within your being. Ever notice how, when you're having a bad day, little things that would typically be beneath your notice bug the crap out of you? That isn't because the energy behind the little thing is suddenly so much bigger, but because your own energy has realigned itself based on the flow of your day.

We have the ability to stand in the face of tremendous adversity, overcome seemingly insurmountable obstacles, turn darkness into beauty, and bring love, compassion, and generosity into a hopeless scenario simply because we choose to do so. Do you think a lit candle, a photograph, a few rose petals, and some carefully chosen words have the power to completely remove a person's control over their own reality bubble? Let me assure you, they don't.

Magick that would remove another's ability to make their own choices will occasionally appear to bring about the desired outcome, but it is an illusion. Whenever you seek to violate a natural law, whether it's gravity or another's ability to choose their own reality, there are repercussions. It's not karma. If you think back to high school science, we learned that energy can neither be created nor destroyed, a concept known as the Law of Conservation of Energy. It's not that you pulled energy from some disconnected cosmic fuel tank to put into your rite; whether you are aware of it or not, it was *your* energy that was put into the spell. If that energy does not find a home (through a harmonious working) it will follow the path of least resistance and return to you.

Wicca has a handy little tool that followers of that path refer to as the Threefold Law. It states, "Whatever you do will return three times to you." This isn't entirely accurate, in my opinion, or reality would quickly be reduced to a mystical checking account where certain actions would add to your balance while other actions would represent a karmic withdrawal. However, it's an extremely useful rule of thumb to use, especially if you're new to magick, when considering the outcome of any working.

Does the target of your affection love you? Like a friend, perhaps, but not in a romantic sense. Will you have to take control of their reality bubble, in other words circumvent their free will, if you make the choice for them where your desires are concerned? Absolutely. Running through a list of questions about the focus of a rite will often reveal the energy behind your working. In this example, you aren't seeking love for yourself, you're seeking to take control of another's free will. If your working fails to find a home - and it will because it violates at least one untouchable principle - that same energy is what will return to you.

What will most likely happen if your working is successful at all? The object of your affection will find they're strangely interested in you and your hopes will soar. Then they will realize that they truly do only love you like a friend - their original position - and the let down from that will seek to overwhelm your own reality bubble with sorrow, grief, and loss. The intent to change how someone else is feeling has returned to you to change how you feel.

WHAT YOU CAN DO

It could be easily said that magick is best worked in harmony with the flow of reality, but that would be somewhat inaccurate. A slightly more accurate statement would be that magick only works in harmony with the flow of reality and that any other approach simply rebounds off the web of manifestation that creates this moment and returns to you. This rebound effect isn't some horrible form of karmic retribution, but simply the Universe's way of saying, "This belongs to you. You put it out there and it doesn't fit; you're welcome to have it back."

A skilled practitioner never attempts to circumvent natural laws, but seeks to understand where a gentle nudge can create the desired change. To use our example of the thrown ball above, while an unexpected gust of wind may not influence our ball's ascent a great deal, that same gust of wind is enough to keep an arrow from hitting its target. Focusing on improving yourself by dealing with your challenges, embracing your own worth, and exploring concepts that help build your confidence may not make your friend love you, but may allow you to discover the true value of their friendship as they stand beside you, encourage you, and cheer you on.

And you never know, as you continue forward on your own path, you may discover a mutual love with someone who is attracted to your new approach to your own life that makes you wonder how you could have ever had a crush on your friend.

Working within the flow of reality makes you a part of the process. We can succinctly frame this approach as "working in balance" but I also tend to refer to it as "flow." Working flow - approaching reality from a position of balance - creates strength, as the harmony allows the natural laws to be secondary and tertiary forces that not only add to your working, but empower your very path. Those same laws that prevent you from working magick from one perspective, can significantly assist your working from a harmonious alignment. The flip side of this particular approach is what I call "control" as it seeks its own desires regardless of where the flow of reality is leading you. Seeking to circumvent natural laws through control creates dissent. Not only does your working lack the additional power of a rite performed in balance, but the existing natural laws, by their very nature, stand against you as you set yourself against their flow. While there are ways of empowering control to the point that it can be an effective approach, it always comes with a significant cost.

Generally speaking (and this is where the other part of Wicca's Threefold Law comes in) each time you work with the flow of reality, you aren't simply avoiding a pitfall, but are actually strengthening your connection to the spirits around you. If all of reality is created from the Divine, then we interact with the sacred in all that we do. Working in flow, harmonizing our workings with the greater weave of reality, not only increases the power in such a working, but lends the energy of our rite to the spirits that are also aligned in the same way. For instance, if you take a ritualistic approach to cleaning up and healing a portion of local ravaged landscape, don't be surprised if the spirits of that place eventually reach out to you. While you probably weren't aware of it, they were already seeking a similar outcome to your own magickal intent. Your working actually empowered and assisted them, which is where the "lends the energy of our rite to the spirits that are also aligned in the same way" comes in. While typically unintended, that connection holds the potential of offering us tremendous benefits on our own path.

Working in harmony isn't simply good mystical manners, it is how we build community with the spirit world. If an acquaintance that I haven't seen for twenty years calls me up and asks me for help, chances are I will see what I can do to assist them; if my best friend calls for help, I'll have them fill me in on the details after I'm standing at their side. Certain aspects of the spirit world approach relationships between us and them in the same way. Your magickal workings will receive a massive boost if you do nothing more than set your ego aside and begin seeking to work in harmony with the flow of reality and the spirits around you.

Don't worry. Learning to approach your magick in such a manner is easier than you might think. In fact, large portions of this book are devoted to exactly that approach.

ACCOMMODATING YOUR PATH

As a general rule of thumb, you can't use magick to create something out of nothing. Want to throw fireballs from your hand like some Hollywood wizard? It isn't going to happen. Want to create vast wealth for yourself, even if it's just by casting a spell to win the lottery? That isn't going to happen either, for a very different reason.

Everything in reality has a journey. An easier way to consider that concept is to accept that everything in all of reality has a story to tell that is uniquely their own. A flame, for example, doesn't simply exist; it needs something to ignite it, fuel to keep it burning, and is subject to countless natural laws. It too has a very simple, very limited, reality bubble. A flame's story may be one of being born when the friction of a matchbook's strike strip ignited the head of the match, of growing as it consumed the wooden matchstick, before a hand, afraid of having its fingers burned, rapidly shook it from existence, leaving only a thin wisp of dissipating smoke in its wake.

Magick cannot circumvent a story for one very simple reason: the Law of Conservation of Energy. To create something without a story is to simply will new energy to appear in a closed system that we call reality. You can only successfully work with flow, not because I think it's a philosophically better option, but because it has the weight of reality behind it. That doesn't mean that your working, no matter how unintentionally misguided, is doomed to failure. Practitioners never make the connection that, six months after they stood in their backyard chanting, "Flame! Flame! Flame!" as they attempted to create fire from nothing, they are suddenly backing away from the fireball that unexpectedly erupted from too much fuel on their barbecue grill.

We live a life divided by calendars, alarm clocks, and closely tended schedules; reality flows from one sunrise to the next, the seasons slowly turning, mountains rising or eroding, and our local star slowly aging. Our approach is in the now; reality's approach is set to a very different clock. And then we wonder why our working didn't happen in what we considered to be a timely manner.

Magick is slow. It rarely happens instantly. It does sometimes, but it's rare. There was a day when I was walking downtown, thinking about a Chinese restaurant that I wanted to tell a friend about and caught myself saying aloud, "I really wish I had a menu," when a paper takeout menu for that very restaurant literally fell out of the sky and landed at my feet. Did it fly out of an office window stories above me? Did the wind carry the menu on some truly unexpected journey from the restaurant on the other side of town? I'll never know. All that I'm truly sure of is that the menu had a journey of its own to tell, if only I knew how to listen. Our working will find a space to manifest in that network of stories in such a way that it adds to the greater tale instead of interrupting or erasing one of the voices that are already present. Magick will typically follow the path of least resistance in order to find that harmonious space, a journey and story of its own that will often take more time than we anticipate our working will require.

One of the things that we often overlook when approaching a working is that not only does the rite need to be in harmony with reality for it to be effective, not only does it need to honor the stories of those the working will interact with, but it needs to honor our own story and our own path.

When you need to heal yourself of a physical injury or disease and want to add a magickal component to that healing, the focus shouldn't be on eliminating the virus, erasing the wound, or destroying the cancer. Approaching things in that manner directs the energy of the rite away from you and into the reality of the malady. Focus instead on resuming your life, on the energy involved in being who you are and embracing the things you'll do *once you're free of the injury or the disease*. That puts the focus of your working not only within your reality bubble, but integrates the power into the healing journey (or story) before you. After all, this is your story - and considering the way that magick flows, when you approach your working in that manner you've already got the weight of reality behind you. Adding a little magickal oomph in that direction simply further empowers the process. The only caveat is if the healing journey itself holds insight and perspective that are critical to your path and would be challenging (at best) to achieve through other means. At that point, the best you can do is simply be present, focus on reaching toward full healing, and take things one moment at a time.

If you're struggling with "fill in the blank," if you really, really want "that thing, that event, that outcome," chances are you're not going to get it through magick. If you could, you'd rob yourself of your own story. Stories are challenging, but overcoming our challenges - especially the hard ones - is where wisdom is earned. We desperately need to stop thinking of wisdom as some touchy-feely characteristic and start thinking of it as mystical currency. Wisdom "buys" us safe passage through challenging portions of our path, it opens deeper perspectives and meaning, it lends us extra strength when we are at our wit's end, and it tells our core self, "I've proven myself ready and able to responsibly wield more power." While few of us can consistently and clearly hear our soul's calling, I guarantee you that it will not discard the opportunity to take some serious steps forward on your path in order to feed your ego's wanton desires. It will, however, do all it can to help you grow and evolve, regardless of what it is that you may want in the moment.

It's not that there is some higher cosmic power that is derailing your working or that you haven't earned enough "good karma" to be deserving of reaping the bounty you seek, it's simply that your core, that still small voice that speaks through your intuition, knows what's the better path for you. Listen to that voice, even if it's just the tiniest nudge, even if you don't like what it has to say in that same, "But Ma, I don't want to eat all my vegetables before I get dessert!" sort of way. If you do, when you look back on that stretch of road, chances are you will begin to see all of the reasons why the harder path was the right one for you to travel.

BEYOND YES AND NO

There's a well-worn philosophical question that people tend to throw around from time to time:
"If you could go back in time and murder Adolf Hitler before he came to power and committed so many atrocities, would you do so?" Killing Hitler at that point in time holds the very real potential of ensuring that the Holocaust never comes to pass and may even go so far as derailing the events that would lead to World War II. All you would have to do is murder an individual who, at that point in his life, had achieved nothing greater than being an increasingly frustrated art student.
The question is designed to encourage debate on morality, ethics, and a number of related topics. Is it okay to kill an innocent before they've committed a crime, even if by doing so you will potentially save millions of lives? Some say, "Yes. The price of murdering one individual is worth saving millions of others." Some say, "No. Murder is wrong, period, and no murder is justified regardless of what the death will achieve." There are countless valid reasons to embrace either perspective. But that question is a very real example of the challenge we face when approaching magick.
We're used to questions that have a concrete answer. If we really want something, the answer is either to get it for ourselves or choose to deny ourselves access to the thing which we desire. When we embrace this perspective, we draw a world for ourselves that is composed mostly of extremes - black and white, right and wrong, go and stop, on

and off. Sometimes there isn't a right answer; or it's a shade of gray; or the best approach is to wait a moment for the scenario before us to clarify itself before we choose a course of action.

And sometimes, the answer is that we need to step outside of the box the question frames for us and get creative with our solution.

Imagine that you went back in time and, instead of murdering Hitler as an innocent young man, you became his closest friend. Rather than having his perspective shaped by the events of his world your friendship molded his worldview instead. Together you bemoaned the critics who assailed his artistic endeavors over a few beers at the local tavern and, instead of letting his anger take root, you encouraged him to rise above the criticism. Sure, maybe his ambitions that were represented by his thwarted artistic career were too big to simply give up on and the path before him called for something larger, but what if instead of going into politics you convinced him to travel the world with you? You'd become world travelers together and his simple sketches of distant lands and peoples, married to your stories of your adventures, would become tremendously popular with both critics and the masses. What if you worked hard, encouraged each other, pooled your money, and began to purchase and sell the works of undiscovered artists that were very similar to the art he once created? As art brokers, you'd praise his artistic eye and the pieces he plucked from obscurity, both of you growing in wealth and esteem in the eyes of the artistic community that once belittled him. There are a thousand paths before both of you as you step into your time machine that lead to places other than war and atrocity and only one of them involves the murder of a still-innocent boy.

To put it simply, the key question where magick is concerned is never, "Yes or no?" The question is always, "Why?"

Why kill a young boy? To stop the deaths of millions. Why would you need to kill him? Because he will one day become a monster. Why does he become a monster? Are there ways to introduce another influence into the mix that would set him upon another path? What could you do that would exert enough influence on his life and on his path that Hitler would end up finding another way?

Remember, the gust of wind may not be enough to change the flight of the ball, but it can make the arrow miss its target. Sometimes, instead of pulling the trigger, all you need to do is raise a beer, dream a dream, and become someone's friend.

One of the fundamental principles of magick, which we'll explore further in the pages ahead, is referred to simply as, "As below, so above." It describes the parallels that exist between mundane and spiritual reality, not only illuminating the path to successful magickal workings, but leading us to the perspective that "All is One." There aren't any mythical-level wizards or sorceresses around today, not because the power is missing, but because their own lives are out of balance. You can't work epic magick if your approach to your own life is stuck in the elementary. There is a very real parallel between the two. Treat the connections in your own life well and magick will flow more freely. Honor the seemingly mundane relationships in your world and the spirit world will respond more readily to your workings.

So, effective magick needs to be worked in harmony with the flow of reality? How do we even begin to understand that flow? Keep reading. That's our next step.

CHAPTER THREE

THE ROAD BEFORE US

Magickal energy exists outside of the flow of linear time. There are techniques to work magick hand-in-hand with past and future versions of yourself which circumvent our typical perspective of time flowing from the past, through the present, and into the future. If you come across a magickal tool or ritual site, even centuries after it participated in the most recent rite, a person who is open to such energies can still sense (and often accurately read) the story told by the item or location. During ritual, time flows in strange patterns; a seemingly short ritual may have taken place over the course of hours and a rite that seemed to take hours may be performed in mere minutes.

Because magick exists outside of the flow of linear time, it must come from a mystical source as every mundane source in our reality is bound by the chains of time. It can't come from a stone, whether it is a beautiful crystal or a simple river rock, as magick is not bound by time and those stones will one day erode away into sand and dust. The energy can't come from a wand or staff, as those tools last less than the blink of an eye from the perspective of eternity. The Earth and moon will one day be engulfed and consumed by an aging sun. Even the sun, our local star, will one day fade away.

In much the same way that peanut butter is made from peanuts or a caress is born from a gentle touch, the qualities of magickal energy must reflect its parent or source. Magick isn't bound by linear time, so it must be timeless; it isn't limited by the mundane, so its parent must be something other than physical; it must embrace a wide spectrum of energy, from emotion to thought, so in a way, the source of magick must also embrace all of reality.

Spirit, in whatever form you choose to define that sacred manifestation, is the only place where such energy could arise.

There are a number of complex, interlocking magickal laws that define the structure of the mystical universe. We understand that even magick must have a story. The energy that we work with in our rites also has a journey of its own. It must have a source that is in harmony with the energy's own journey, balanced from origin to destination. In its own way, this means that magickal energy also has its own "reality bubble" and that it has a story of its own to tell. While we can bend the energy to our will, while we can raise it, ground it, direct it, and apply it, we can't change the fundamental nature of magickal energy. To embrace all of these concepts and more, such energy would have to come from a source that isn't limited by the framework of our mundane world.

When we draw energy from the earth or the sky, we're not pulling from a reserve of energy that is held by those physical sources. If we did so, the tree or stone we drew the energy from would be consumed in much the same way we release the energy of wood by the use of a flame. What we're doing when we pull energy from a physical focus object, even something on the same scale as the earth beneath our feet or the rolling ocean before us, is pulling from the source that the earth or the ocean is connected to and using the physical manifestation (the sea, for instance) as a focus to filter that energy into a particular flavor so that it's easier for us to work with. In other words, we don't pull energy *from* a crystal; we pull it *through* a crystal, using the stone as a filter to change the resonance of energy before it reaches our hands.

The source that we're drawing through our physical object, even if that object is as expansive as the earth or sky, is Spirit.

For Spirit to work in this manner, it has to be omnipresent, existing everywhere simultaneously, connected to everything, uniting everything. The deeper we step into magick and mysticism, the more that we realize that this energy, the very essence of Spirit, is literally everywhere and everything, a concept that I often describe as "All is One."

If something were to exist outside of Spirit, then by that very concept, it would be elevated to a level equal to Spirit. And if it is true that everything is unified ("All is One"), then whenever we experience separation or division it simply indicates that we have yet to refine our perception far enough that we have reached the origin of that energy.

Think about it this way.

Let's say that in the vast expanse of everything, the entire expanse of reality is Spirit. There is nothing else, because Spirit is all encompassing; it is, literally, everything. Now imagine that next to Spirit, separate from it, is a bowl of oatmeal. On one hand, we have Spirit. On the other, we have oatmeal. In all of reality, they are the only two things in existence.

Because these are the only two things that have definition in all of reality - and because they are separate from each other - then they are only reflections of a bigger, all-encompassing concept. After all, something has to encompass both Spirit and the oatmeal. If we can say, "There's Spirit and next to Spirit is this bowl of oatmeal," then something bigger contains them both. Whether we refer to that larger concept as the Universe, nothingness, or by some other name, it is a clear sign that an additional level exists beyond the current limits of our perception. Even when we reach a place where we can't go any farther, when all that exists is Spirit, we may one day discover – as our understanding deepens and our perception encompasses more of reality – that the path goes even farther, ever deeper, and there is infinitely more to discover on the path before us.

What we have learned so far is that each time we drop defining labels and release our preconceived ideas, the landscape before us becomes a little more unified. Instead of blaming a particular race, gender, or political group for an unwanted situation, we understand that the struggle before us is a human creation. Without the labels, we stop pointing fingers; without the need to assign blame, we allow those involved in the scenario to be something more than just the root of the problem.

While this may seem like a very humanitarian way of approaching interpersonal relationships, our interactions with others and the world around us are the building blocks of our mystical practice as defined by "As below, so above." Likewise, this same principle illustrates the concept of "All is One."

It's often a bit easier to understand if we reverse the flow and look at things from the opposite direction. Imagine that there is a group of naked men standing on the right and a group of naked women standing on the left. It's often challenging to understand their unity when we can clearly see the physical differences of the two genders. The key is to understand that those two groups are an *artificial construct*. They didn't suddenly appear in a gender-divided groups; someone sorted them into such. Someone - whether it was the naked test subjects themselves or a mysterious third party - said, "Okay, men, over on the right; women, over there on the left. C'mon! Let's go. We need to divide you into groups."

While there are countless reasons why artificial constructs are created, the key is in that term itself. First of all, they are artificial; in other words, they are not a naturally occurring process and do not reflect their origin. Second, they are a construct; someone took the raw materials (in this case, human beings) and chose to create a division (in our example, one based entirely on gender).

Whenever we encounter a division, we are not looking at the source. While it is immensely useful to use specific characteristics or attributes in magickal workings - such as the phase of the moon or the properties of the Element of Fire - these divisions themselves are artificial constructs. That doesn't make them a bad thing. A construct can be a weapon ("You can't do that because you fit this label") and it can also be a tool.

As we apply this concept, removing labels and seeking unity, we eventually come to a point where there is only one thing in all of existence and it manifests in such a manner that it cannot be defined by a label. It is at that point that we are presented with the concept of Spirit or "All is One" or whatever shorthand we choose to use that describes an indescribable reality. That's also where the biggest secret in magick can be found. It's not that we draw the energy for our rites and our magick directly from "God" - it's that, because Spirit is absolutely everything, because "All is One," once we drop our need for separation and division we encounter a simple yet very powerful truth - we are "God."

When we are incarnated into this reality, we accept certain limitations to our ability to perceive the Divine. It's the only way that this level of reality can work. By limiting our perception of reality, by giving up our understanding that everything, including us, is "God," our focus narrows down to our own wants and needs. This allows us to experience all of the things we incarnated into this lifetime to learn. Our illusionary challenges don't feel so illusionary when we toss fear into the mix. Likewise, our divinity doesn't seem quite so powerful in the face of our doubt when we second-guess ourselves. As beings of Love, we would never step deeper into that love if we never had to set aside anger or hurt and choose a loving response instead. If we retained the perspective that we're Spirit and that all things are part of the divine whole, we would not only fail to experience fear, anger, and the other negative emotions that spur us toward growth, but we wouldn't be so creative in manifesting this reality.

With each step forward we take in our spiritual growth, we also take another step toward understanding the sacred nature of all reality. With an increased understanding, our limitations fall away a little more. As our limitations fall away, we access more power. With more power, we wield more magick and are presented with new lessons. Our new lessons challenge us to take another step forward in our spiritual growth. And this continues in an endless cycle.

That is one of the key reasons why I stress personal and spiritual growth so much on the path I teach. You can conduct all of your rites in ancient languages, memorize arcane texts, and do fundamentally perfect rituals and still not achieve the level of power you can by simply learning and growing, developing the capacity to show love and compassion, and taking the steps that lead you to an ever deeper understanding that All is One. The thing about magick is that we need to understand the relationship between our finite mundane existence and our greater, limitless spiritual identity in order to engage in an active role in creating our own reality. The most powerful tool in our mystical toolbox is truly understanding that there are no limits to what we can achieve - and, ironically, that's one of the hardest lessons for us to learn.

As we navigate our paths, each of us picks up bits of wisdom and insight along the way. With these tools in hand, we address not only the challenges we face, but their existence allows us to begin to form our personal mythologies. Those of us who pray believe that our chosen definition of the Divine will hear us. Those of us who strike out on our own believe that we have the necessary tools within ourselves to overcome our challenges. Through our lessons and the understanding of our own answers we each develop a unique system of belief. Some of us hold onto those beliefs for a lifetime; others outgrow them from time to time and shed them like a snake sheds its skin.

My own path has led me through various religions and approaches to spirituality. It may seem like a contradiction that a practitioner of magick would admire the example of the Christian Jesus or that a shaman would rely on the teachings of Buddha in navigating his path. To me, the contradiction only appears when we look too closely at the details, fixate on the labels, and miss the bigger picture.

Think about it this way. Imagine that a brilliant artist had painted a masterpiece so large that it covered the entire wall of an art museum. In this example, we aren't just students of life, spirituality, and magick; we're also art students. Each of us scrutinizes the massive painting, trying to understand the artist's intent and how it parallels our own lives. As we approach the canvas, because of its immense dimensions, we begin to lose perspective. And as we move as close as we can without touching the painting, all we can see are individual brush strokes and a small portion of the colors used in the overall painting.

Now imagine that the painting represents spirituality. Because of our limited perspective, standing as close as we are to our own path, each of us sees only a tiny portion of the entire picture. What's more is that we tend to play it safe and stick to our portion of the painting, to the comfort of our own spiritual practice, allowing us to see only the brush strokes and colors that are right in front of us.

When we stand so close to the painting, those individual brush strokes take on an unintended importance. To one who stands in a place where the brush strokes moved in a horizontal direction, that motion tends to not only take on an implied sacred correctness, but it is also challenged by the person who stands so close to a portion of the painting where the paint was applied with vertical brushstrokes. Rather than recognizing that our own perspective is limited and accepting another's observations as a gift from portions of the painting we can't see, we begin to argue about who is right and who is wrong. We lose sight of the concept that the painting is much bigger than we will ever perceive and only by finding the common ground in each of our perspectives will we ever be able to understand more than what awaits us just in front of our nose.

Part of my own practice involves stepping back and trying to see more of the painting than I could see the day before. Not only does it assist me as a spiritual teacher, but it adds a holistic understanding to my personal path and what I practice on my own. Instead of seeing individual portions of the painting, I look for how one portion blends into the other and how the colors deepen and fade to make light and shadow, to add richness to the painting. While I certainly haven't mastered the concept, one of the things that I work with on my path is learning to see how the various portions of spirituality flow together. In our example of the painting, I'm slowly learning to step farther and farther back and embrace more of the composition rather than focusing on individual brush strokes.

In doing so, my tools have changed. As I've let go of more and more of the specifics and looked instead to the flow of life, my path, and the world around me, things have become simplified. That's why the contradictions fall away. The guidelines that I rely on to navigate my path have been reduced to four simple rules. At first glance, this may seem like nothing more than the philosophy that I use in my own personal growth, but what I've learned is that our paths are all part of a single canvas. All is One. By embracing the following concepts, I've also learned to step deeper into the mystical aspects of my path and have added an incredible depth and power to my energy work, rituals, and magick.

Rule #1: We're in School

The first thing we need to remember is that we're not perfect. I embrace the concept of reincarnation and believe that we're here to learn and grow, a process that I once heard coined as spiritual alchemy. Where an alchemist of yore would seek to transmute one material into another, we seek to evolve our own souls, growing over lifetimes from a spiritual infant to a wise spiritual elder.

What that means to us is that we're going to face challenges. Our boundaries are going to be pushed. We're going to find ourselves stretched beyond our comfort zones. The understanding behind that concept is that we will occasionally not only fail to get a perfect score, but that from time to time we're going to fall flat on our faces.

If we learn to understand the fabric of our own lives as seen through the lens of our spiritual paths, we come to realize that there is a lesson to be learned in each moment. We learn that falling and picking ourselves up to try again is where strength, perseverance, and wisdom are forged. We discover that our challenges make us stronger, that they allow us to let go of concepts and filters that hold us back. And with the combination of both strength and freedom, we find ourselves stepping deeper and deeper into the heart of our paths.

Rule #2: We're In Charge

It's obvious that this is your life. You make the choices. You live each moment. In every conceivable way, this life is yours to live. It's surprising how many people fail to grasp that simple concept. If your life was a movie, you would be the star. If your life was a concert, you'd be the one standing at center stage. You aren't cast in a supporting role in the story of your life - it is truly all about you.

This means that you get to say no and either draw boundaries or walk away. It means that you get to say yes even when the joy or opportunity before you seems frivolous or something that someone told you that you weren't good enough to do. Each new scene in the story of you is being written by the star - and you, dear reader, are firmly entrenched in that starring role.

What we often fail to realize is that the concept goes far beyond the moment we live in and the tangible things we can write down on a sheet of paper. How do we accurately define love? How do you explain the calling of your intuition that you can't put into words? Because this is school and because we literally manifest our own reality, life specifically weaves itself for our benefit. Literally. That isn't "for our pleasure" or "for our enjoyment," but for our benefit. This process isn't directed by our immediate wants or needs but by what we refer to as our soul or spirit or higher self. It wants to grow and evolve regardless of how much our limited perspective may want to simply avoid the whole situation. However, if you approach life as school and begin to understand the lessons that unfold before you, you also begin to realize that it all happens for a reason.

The next step in the evolution of that concept is to understand that you create it all. That doesn't mean that you are responsible for the hardships or traumas that you experience, but that you're strong enough to overcome each and every one of them. Even in the darkest night of the soul, there is not only wisdom and strength to be claimed, but the promise that the sun will rise once more. And when you reach the point that you know, to the core of your being, that you are manifesting your reality, suddenly your magick and the options before you are without limit.

The key is to remember that manifesting your reality is not the same as being solely responsible for all of the bad things that happened to you. Those are not your fault and are not your responsibility. This concept is easiest to understand if you imagine that you're an artist who sculpts with wood. Some of the wood you're given is perfectly seasoned with a beautiful color and grain; some of the wood is pitted, knotted, and even rotten. The state of the wood is not the artist's responsibility; what the artist manifests is found solely in what they do with the wood once it arrives in their hands. The act of manifestation is not found in taking responsibility for the challenge that has appeared in your path. If "All is One" and every moment is sacred, then that challenge has a journey (and manifestation) of its own. Manifesting your own reality isn't what appears in your hands, but what you do with those things once they appear. You aren't responsible for a hurricane that levels your neighborhood; the reality you manifest is how you keep yourself and your loved ones sheltered during the storm, how you rebuild, and how you reach out to the others in your community who are in need.

RULE #3: IT'S BIGGER THAN YOU REALIZE

The biggest hindrance in this entire process is that we are constantly limiting what reality can be. Speaking even to experienced practitioners of magick, you'll hear phrases like "magick doesn't work that way". Simply remember that to every rule, there's an exception. To every guideline, there's a loophole. This isn't because we can ethically violate certain concepts or subvert natural laws but because reality is infinitely bigger than we imagine it to be. That's not "reality is infinitely big." For even the most open-minded of us, reality isn't just bigger than we imagine it; it's infinitely bigger than our wildest imaginings.

There are no limitations to this concept, just principles in place that structure our learning environment and what we experience. For instance, if you stood outside and looked up at the sky, your natural inclination is to believe that you can't fly. In fact, it was a commonly held belief for centuries that man would never take to the air. While we can achieve flight here on Earth, it requires us to overcome the force of gravity to do so. In all of our workings there is always a journey to be completed or a story to be told.

All of the challenges before us can be overcome. The key is finding what we need to do in order to succeed in that endeavor. For instance, there are different ways to achieve flight. We can raise energy (such as in winged flight where lift exceeds weight), shift our energy to another vibration (by adopting wings such as with a hang glider), or by becoming lighter than air (such as with a hot air balloon.) We do the same thing on our spiritual paths. We raise energy when we work magick. We shift our energy to another vibration, such as in shamanic journeying. And we achieve the parallel of lighter than air flight by letting go of the things that hold us to our spiritual ground.

Just remember, it was once believed that man would never take to the air. What do you really long for in your own life that you believe is beyond your reach? Our limitations are only what we allow them to be.

RULE #4: THE SECRET IS LETTING GO

The secret key behind mysticism, magick, and spiritual growth isn't to amass knowledge, memorize incantations, or adhere blindly to ancient philosophies. If it is only our own preconceived ideas that limit what we can achieve and who we can be, then whenever we release our fear and need for control, we also release our limitations. Magick as I teach it is free form, free flowing, and, simply put, works. I've watched the sea physically respond to my words, surging high above my head or parting around where I stood in the surf. Candles have reignited before my eyes. Spirits have physically manifested in my rites. And, during shamanic work along a wild stretch of coastline, my footsteps literally disappeared from the sand.

Does this make me special? Is it a level that only a few people can reach? Not at all. Through an application of the four simple guidelines introduced above, each of us

can reach a level on our paths that will exceed our wildest
dreams, that will bring us inner peace, and will fill our lives
with love.

Within spiritual circles, we seek to understand not
only our own internal landscape, but the influence of the
subtle realms around us. We hear terms like "the astral plane"
or "the spirit realm" or, as I like to call it, "the Elsewhere." We
hear other people's thoughts, follow our own intuition, and
have dreams and visions of events before they take place.
But that's not all. We do work in the Dreamtime, we exercise
our "psychic" abilities, and we manifest reality, somehow
distinguishing between magick, miracles, and plain ol'
coincidence.

Countless volumes have been written on the
distinctions between telepathy and empathy, between the
astral and ethereal realms. Ask one question, receive one
thousand answers, each bringing additional questions of
their own.

Thankfully, it's actually much simpler than all of that.

In my own practice, through countless experiments
and exercises on my own and with classrooms full of seekers,
I've been able to organize all of the above into three categories.
And to make this process as easy as possible, I refer to those
categories as Level 1, Level 2, and, you guessed it, Level 3.

One of the concepts that we miss, especially
within the confines of our culture, is that we live a layered
experience. Your mind can be thinking one thing, your body
responding through its own automatic processes, and your
intuition chiming in with a third opinion. As very few of
us are trained to develop an awareness of these sometimes
conflicting voices, most of us learn to ignore the vast majority
of the data that we constantly receive from the universe.
What happens is that we shut out a wealth of information
and live an existence that is unintentionally limited.

As unlikely as it seems, everything within and beyond
our potential experiences, from psychic phenomena to the
written word, fits neatly into one of these three categories.
What's more is that an understanding of how these levels
interact and how they are woven together provides us with
tremendous insight into the workings of the mystical world.
This insight isn't an untested theory; experience has shown

that it lends itself to being used as a tool to unravel processes and gain access to deeper and deeper levels of spiritual reality. Rather than separating our experiences into dividing labels, I like to use this approach to show how our perceptions of various events and phenomena integrate together into a seamless whole.

LEVEL ONE

At its heart, Level One is "any contained linear phenomena that's doesn't rely on symbolism for meaning." Mathematics is the ultimate example of Level One. If you take the equation "2 + 2," it will always equal "4." Level One is a linear process. You can draw a direct line between the phenomena and it's product - just like you can in a math equation.

The written word is another example of Level One phenomena. Once you've written the words on a page, they don't tend to change unless you edit them, either removing words or adding new words in a concrete, linear fashion.

Level One does have what could actually be considered psychic abilities - namely hearing, touch, taste, and sight. Think about it this way: we're reading the words on this page with our eyes, but our eyes aren't physically touching the letters. While we don't consider sight to be a psychic ability because we understand it, can measure the phenomena, and can both start and stop it (such as wearing or removing a blindfold), psychic abilities tend to bridge perceived gaps. We can hear a person's thoughts even though we need to cross the gap created by their silence to do so; we can glean information about previous events from an object by bridging the gap between the present and the past; we can gain insight into coming events by bridging the gap between the present and the future. Sight allows us to experience an object even though we aren't physically touching that object, however it does so in a measurable linear fashion. While we don't think of the ability to see as a psychic ability, it qualifies as one on Level One, which itself is a very linear realm.

The way that magick tends to work, when we one day understand the process behind phenomena such as telepathy and precognition, new doors will open for us. As our understanding of those abilities turns them into linear concepts (Level One) new abilities will emerge on Levels Two and Three to take their place. It's one of the beautiful structures built into physical reality: no matter how far your path may take you, there are always new landscapes to explore.

LEVEL TWO

Each step deeper into our perceived experiences releases more and more of the linear nature of reality. Level Two is our first real experience with that. This is the home of what we term classic psychic phenomena. It's where magick takes place. On Level Two we experience telepathy, intuition, precognition. It's here that we connect with energy, where symbols are empowered and where dreams take place.

The secret is that we don't need any occult techniques, arcane phrases, or mastery of any particular ability to access each and every experience on Level Two. We experience them all the time. Somewhere along the way (and it looks like it happens about the time we start school and begin focusing so strongly on rote education which shifts our focus to Level One), we simply start tuning out experiences and input from Level Two. It doesn't disappear. We don't lose it. We simply focus so completely on other areas that we forget that it's there.

Believe it or not, experiencing life from a Level Two perspective is actually pretty easy to understand. One of the examples that I use in the classes that I teach is horseback riding. If you've ever spent time on a horse, you know that if you try to control the horse by pulling on the reins and approaching it through cause and effect (Level One) approach, the horse will fight you every step of the way. However, there's a moment when you and the horse become in sync. At that moment, you can feel the horse's intent, its personality, and the two of you begin to interact on an entirely different level - one that if we were doing it with another human being, we would instantly define as "telepathic." That's Level Two - and you didn't need an ounce of training to reach it.

We pick up on Level Two all the time. It simply doesn't register in a mind that's been wired to embrace Level One. When I work with new students, we go through a process that allows people to perceive their innate ability to connect with and really feel the energy around them. It takes all of forty-five seconds of instruction to begin the process· and reconnect with the input you receive on Level Two. This isn't a new ability; it's as simple as saying, "Can you feel the floor beneath your feet?" We rapidly expand to the point where the attendees can sense energy, define the difference between multiple energy sources, and intuitively read the world around them.

And then I point out specific examples of energy sources from their daily lives and how different each feels. "Notice how different your bedroom at home feels from the shopping mall or the beach or a long soak in the tub." The students in the class nod in agreement. And then I remind them that those energy sources aren't present in our classroom, that the students know how each feels because they've always been able to sense them. In other words, they're calling forth the memory of what those energy sources felt like, a process that goes on in the background, simply overlooked by our conscious minds. The students are accessing a pool of experiences that they had without knowing it. Those experiences simply didn't consciously register in a mind that has been heavily wired for linear thought.

LEVEL THREE

Each level has its own language. The farther the jump between levels, the harder it is to "translate." For instance, we can use the written word (Level One) to pretty accurately describe Level Two and the things that take place on that level. However, it's much more challenging to use the same written word to describe Level Three - simply because there's a two level jump in between. It's also why people who filter everything through Level One have a difficult time believing in miracles and the like - it's a two level jump in the opposite direction.

The easiest way to understand Level Three is this: if you think of Level One as "manifestation based on a linear process, then Level Three is "manifestation without a linear process." It's how things "just happen" in our world. It's manifestation on an rather amazing level. It's how, much to the discomfort of three doctors and an orthopedic specialist, my severely damaged knee with two hideously torn ligaments and shredded cartilage was completely healed without surgery over a period of ten days.

Level Three, simply put, is miracles. It's raw, unexpected emotion. It's intense sexual chemistry. It's primal, powerful, raw - all of which is the very fabric of creation.

Where inner work (for instance, dreaming) on Level Two uses linear form rich with symbolism, Level Three relies on symbolism without form for its language. Chances are you've experienced this, but it's such a big jump from Level Three to Level One (where it would register in your conscious mind) that you don't clearly remember it. You might be picking something up in your intuition right now, but that's Level Two filling in the gaps.

So we use sexual chemistry as an illustration of Level Three, mostly because everyone has experienced it at some point. Remember, Partner A? You were in love, things were good, and sex was an intimate experience that left you feeling warm and loved, wanted and desired, and at home as you curled up in each other's arms in the afterglow. Remember Partner B? You trembled when they were near. You don't ever remember being that aroused. When you made love, you swore the world around you disappeared - not symbolically, but part of you somehow remembers that it actually faded away until all that was left was the two of you. You may have never loved them, but, "WOW!" talk about chemistry!

Partner B is an example of a Level Three connection. We can't explain it, at least not in Level One's linear language. But if we find someone else that's experienced it, we can talk about it in, "You know?" and "Uh-huh," and nothing is really said in linear Level One words because the core of the conversation is taking place on Level Two.

And that's key. We relate to each other, the spirit realm, and the world around us on all three levels all the time. We instinctively and intuitively (Level Two) navigate our world. We literally have conversations with people, especially those that are close enough to us that we're "open" with them, on all three levels simultaneously. What's interesting is that, as you begin to remember to be aware of the connection, you suddenly realize that you're aware that your conversations and interactions take place on multiple levels simultaneously.

Some afternoon, you and a close friend will be spending the day together and lunch will be drawing near. Before you know it, you'll be in the kitchen, you're making sandwiches while they're putting together a salad, and you realize that neither of you suggested it was time for lunch. Neither of you stopped and divided the tasks before you. The key is that it didn't simply happen; while you were chatting away on Level One all kinds of conversations were taking place between you and your close friend on Level Two. It happens all the time - we simply aren't aware of it.

Think of the person who seemed really nice but annoyed you for reasons you can't explain. Or meeting eyes with a stranger in a crowd and both of you communicating with an open smile that says something very different from, "I'm embarrassed to have made eye contact with a stranger." You'll be having a conversation with someone and they'll say they're doing fine, but the communication on Level Two tells you that they're heartbroken even though they're smiling and their eyes are clear. With all three levels going, it's impossible to lie as deception is a product of Level One. Approaching life in this manner, our interactions become incredibly honest. Community spontaneously forms. People are knit together. And abilities that we consider "mystical," "magickal," or "psychic" begin to simply appear in every moment of our daily lives.

The key is, this isn't mystical. It's not magick, at least not in the traditional sense of the word. It's who we are as spiritual beings living life from a physical perspective. That's why, when a knowledgeable teacher can shift our perspective so that we remember what it's like to consciously connect with one of the levels, we're immediately aware of it. It's not just our birthright; it's who we are.

Now imagine what your magickal workings are like when you're aware of all three Levels and able to focus each of them on the ritual at hand.

The only caveat to this process is when someone has experienced a great deal of trauma in their world - especially emotional trauma. Our normal response is to put blocks in place - energetic walls that hold the full weight of the trauma at bay. In our culture, we even refer to it being "shut off" or "walled up," one of the countless examples of our awareness of the Levels trickling through into seemingly mundane life. Unfortunately, we put those walls up in moments of extreme duress - a space where there are intense levels of emotional energy in play - and without the same level of power at our fingertips to bring them down, we have to go through a lengthy process to lower the walls once we choose to do so. There's a small percentage of people who "don't experience" the energy work that I teach. A very small percentage. Everyone else in class can even feel the energy that the closed off person is projecting - it's just that the person can't feel it flowing in either direction. Without exception, depending on what they can or cannot sense, doing nothing more than relying on the information present through an awareness of the three Levels, I can tell them their history on the spot. The Levels and their interaction briefly outlined above are that clearly connected. And if the wound can be found, the healing can begin.

Why divide our experiences into three Levels? Because it allows us to approach them in manageable pieces and manageable pieces can be used as tools. Tools allow us to directly interact with a concept and offer us additional insight into the material at our fingertips. The key behind this process is a principle that I refer to as "the flip side of the coin." This principle is key to unraveling the sacred mysteries that await all around us. When I teach paganism (with a little "p"), what I'm reaching for is that innate spirituality that we would find if we woke up with amnesia on a desert island. We wouldn't find scriptures or a sacred text; we wouldn't memorize correspondences; what we would find is an innate human experience. Themes would emerge. As we learned to see beyond the merely physical into the deeper weave of reality, we'd discover magick.

After all, some sort of magick is practiced by every culture on Earth.

Eventually, we'd uncover a series of principles that we would rely upon in our workings, not because someone told us they were the right way to do things, but because they actually brought about the intended result. One of those concepts is what I refer to as "the flip side of the coin." If energy flows one direction through a structure or concept, then energy can flow in the opposite direction through that same concept or structure.

The concept is fairly simple. If you put a wall up to keep bad things out, that wall will also keep good things out. If a harsh word causes pain, a kind word can heal. As one of my teachers so eloquently put it, "You can't work weal [good] if you don't know how to work woe [bad]." It's not a blank check to justify causing harm, but a deep understanding of how a wound is created tends to shine additional light into the journey of how to fully heal that injury. It's the whole concept of the wounded healer, the reality that we are composed of both shadow and light, and that sometimes the seasons bring life with Spring and Summer and sometimes they bring death with Fall and Winter.

The flip side of the coin teaches us that if we can receive energy through the three Levels, we can also project it through all three. Miracles don't simply happen on Level Three, we can direct them to manifest. Dreaming on Level Two isn't just a world where we're a passive observer, but one where we can be an active participant.

This is why spiritual growth is so fundamental to working effective, powerful magick. The deeper we access the parts of ourselves that allow us to connect with all three Levels, the more power we can access. This isn't just a process where we become happy, whole, and live fully in the moment, but the flip side of that coin is that we learn to raise, project, direct, and manifest massive amounts of magickal power through the exact same process. One side of the coin simply does not exist without the other.

CHAPTER FOUR

SEEING BEYOND ILLUSIONS

Because we chose to accept certain illusions that limit who we truly are, we aren't aware of the vast amount of information, wisdom and energy that are readily available to us. The first step in this process is to discover the appropriate doorway, either by searching on our own or with the assistance of a teacher, behind which can be found a greater portion of reality than we currently have access to and then initiate the intent to step through that door. The key to this process is the understanding that once we have stepped through that doorway, the only thing that is limiting us from immediately accessing the energy that doorway holds (without employing rituals, symbolism or tools to engage with the energy that is now all around us), are the limitations that we choose to place upon ourselves.

The tools, techniques and philosophy are intended to fall away as we grow. We aren't building strength that will fade unless we continually train, but are letting go of illusionary limitations that, once released, no longer have any hold over us. This process may be easier for you to understand if you think of it as being similar to our ability to physically maneuver through the mundane world. As an infant, there is a significant challenge involved in simply developing the strength, coordination and balance to make our body respond to our will. With practice and determination, we learn to roll over. From there, we learn to first crawl, then walk. In a very short time, we are running, skipping, jumping, climbing trees – a wide range of tasks that, as a tiny infant, were not only beyond our ability, but actions whose existence we had yet to even consider when we began our journey. At no point in time did we have to go back and revisit skills in order to move to the next level. Once we learned to run, we no longer had to practice crawling – the ability became a part of who we are, rather than a building block that we needed to constantly employ in order to move on to more advanced forms of movement.

On the path that I teach, our approach to magick and spirituality follows exactly the same progression. We learn skills that are vital for us to access a certain level of reality or reveal a specific spiritual truth, but we then find that we do not need to continually relearn and reapply those skills. Once we understand and believe that we've reached a specific milepost on our journey, that point of our path becomes a part of who we are. Our focus can be on moving as far ahead as our self-imposed limitations will allow us to travel, not on devoting more and more time and energy to portions of the journey that we've already covered.

The key is in understanding the process inherent in the type of existence that we've chosen to live. As human beings there are two critical stages to our physical existence, an existence that, for most of us, will span multiple incarnations or lifetimes. The first stage is learning to find our reason for existing and by honoring that reason, actively engaging in a process of learning to live a life where we are at peace and filled with love - and typically manifest a great deal of joy. The second stage is deciding to reach beyond that first lesson and consciously begin the process of spiritual evolution, a cycle of growth that will enable us to reclaim the perspective that we are divine and leave the need to incarnate into this physical realm behind us.

When you rewind time back to just before the beginning of everything, to the instant before reality was born, there is no physical world. The only thing that exists is spiritual energy. Another way to think about this concept is by playing the "ancestor game." You start with yourself and say, "I came from my parents." Then you say, "My parents came from their grandparents" and name them. It quickly becomes a much easier task if you take one branch of the rapidly expanding tree and follow it back as far as you can go. Eventually, you'll run out of names, which speeds up the game considerably. You can then focus on the species level, rather than the individual. Then, even the species falls away and you reach the building blocks of life. At some point the game draws to a close as the logical mind can't navigate any farther back. Usually this is around the time you reach "cosmic dust cloud" or some variation on the theme if you believe in evolution (if you don't, you reach this point much more rapidly). The step beyond that initial building block can only be described as Spirit as you've reached the moment where there is nothing else to give birth to the physical. Beyond that point, the physical simply doesn't exist. When you reverse the game, you realize that all life, that all of existence came from this spiritual energy.

By its very definition, all of existence is Spirit.

What is asked of you on this path is to not only make that leap and understand reality from this perspective, but you are asked to begin to see the weave that the fabric of life is formed with and learn how to insert your own threads into that cosmic tapestry. You do it all the time. All of reality does. The key is that, by walking this path, you are choosing to insert those threads consciously with an understanding of the implications behind your actions. You're making a statement that you're willing to open your eyes, that you're ready to wake up and step into your role as an incarnated human being and a spiritual entity.

So how do we begin?

Back in the early 1990's, I found myself in much the same place you're at right now. I was working with a wonderful teacher of Native American descent who had agreed to take me on as a student a short time earlier, a relationship that would last for the better part of two years. She lived on one side of the United States, I was on the other, and we corresponded through letters and packages and she recorded her teachings on audio cassette before entrusting them to the postal service. My teacher would give me concepts and theory and send me out to find my own techniques and applications. I was instructed that the lesson wouldn't be completed until I'd successfully navigated through the material and found my own methods for interacting with nature and the spirit world.

Nowadays, that's commonplace in my world, but back then it was a concept that required me to stretch far beyond my comfort zone. I was a little bit in awe of studying with a woman who had been trained by her People's shaman and who was offering to train me as well. I didn't want to screw up. I had no idea what the correct answer should be, what I would find when I slipped out into nature, or if I would somehow meet her expectations of me as her student or fall dreadfully short.

Her first lesson seemed simple enough. I was to go outdoors and sit, quietly, for at least fifteen minutes and simply observe. The exercise would be implemented over the course of thirty consecutive days. If I missed even a single day, the days were reset and the exercise was restarted from the very beginning.

I don't know about you, but I'm a bit of a procrastinator and not always that open to change. To make things worse, I lived in an apartment in the middle of town. I had to work five days a week. There were chores to accomplish; television shows to watch; a thousand distractions beckoned that would keep me from my appointed task.

I was sitting in my living room, watching television late one evening when the assigned exercise slipped into my mind and refused to leave. It was all I could think about, the urge to complete the task so insistent that I was having a difficult time watching the evening's prime time programming. Back in those days, I was even more stubborn and clueless than I am now and it seemed as if the spirit world often needed to strike my head soundly with an ethereal rubber mallet in order to get my attention. Annoyed that the thought wouldn't leave me alone, I leapt up from my chair, grabbed my coat, and slipped outside.

The problem was, I had no idea where I was going. There I was, standing in front of my apartment door, wondering where I could find nature. I could see some trees in the distance, but it was dark and cold and I wasn't about to walk that far. The idea that I could climb in the car and drive to the mountains, forests, or beaches of my native Oregon hadn't even entered my consciousness at this point in my path.

So I did what any complete and utterly clueless novice would do.

I looked around the apartment complex, scanning the darkness for neighbors and checking once more for the headlights of passing cars.

Then I sprinted across the parking lot and slipped into the bushes, crouching within them in the cold and dark, hoping that no one could see me.

When you live in the midst of a media culture, fifteen minutes seems like an eternity. That first night I learned that it's very cold in Oregon in late September. I discovered that passing cars are actually quite loud, especially when you're certain that it's a neighbor returning from the grocery store and that they'll soon be staring at you as you're captured by their headlights. I learned that fifteen minutes seems like three hours, especially when you check your watch every ninety seconds or so. Finally, with an audible sigh of relief, I realized that the fifteen minutes had passed. Carefully checking once more for cars or neighbors, I climbed out of the bushes and dashed back across the parking lot, slipping into the warmth of my apartment and the gentle glow of the beckoning television.

And then I realized that I had twenty-nine more evenings to go.

I was sure that this was one of those things that teachers subjected new students to, an opportunity to test how serious they were about their path and whether they were worthy of the instruction. At that point in my path, I simply couldn't see another reason for sitting outside for two minutes, let alone fifteen minutes for thirty consecutive days. But I wasn't about to give up. If nothing else, I had a stubborn streak a mile wide. When the next evening came, I once more checked the parking lot and then dashed to my sanctuary in the bushes.

Things did not improve. On that second night I realized that, while it's cold in Oregon during late September, it's infinitely more so when it's raining. With an unpleasant mixture of annoyance and disgust, I discovered that even a light sprinkle will drip from leaves and branches for what seemed like hours. That hard-packed dirt will magically turn to mud with only a tiny amount of moisture. That what had seemed like an impossible amount of time to quietly wait the night before simply became an eternity the second time out with the addition of a cold drizzle.

The next evening I found myself firmly planted in front of the television, watching as the digital clock on the VCR informed me of the increasing lateness of the hour. I kept telling myself, "One more show, just one more," until not only had the majority of the evening passed, but it was well-past my normal bedtime.

Reluctantly prying myself from the couch and retrieving my coat, I once more made the dash across the parking lot and slipped into the bushes. I found the same trunk that I had leaned against the previous night and the same hole in the foliage overhead that alternately displayed the stars or let in the rain.

And that was when it finally began to make sense to me. It wasn't just a bush on the side of the parking lot. It was my bush. There was a familiarity to its presence. I knew the trunk that supported my back, the gap in the branches and leaves that showed me the night sky, the patterns of shadows and light formed by its branches and leaves. Somehow, in the middle of the city, huddled under a bush at the edge of my apartment's parking lot, a new world began to open for me. There was a pattern to how the soil softened under the touch of the rain and then slowly grew firm again as the water was drawn to where it would be most useful. I could see the wind as it blew through distant trees and learned to anticipate the moment that it would then dance with the leaves of my own bush. I discovered the beauty in the way light was captured by the sap suspended on the branch before my eyes. My suburban world suddenly became populated by wildlife that I had somehow remained unaware of until that night and I found myself marveling at the rustling sound of sleeping birds perched in the bushes around me.

As the days continued to pass, I found myself looking forward to my time spent in my odd version of nature. And as I slowly learned to observe, an entirely new world opened up for me. I realized that I could feel the plant life around me, not by physical touch, but with something else, something that had always existed inside of me. It was as if my own being extended beyond my body and I could feel where other energies touched it or where they existed beyond the boundaries that I used to define myself. As I sat there quietly, the minutes slowly ticking by, I realized that I could sense the world around me, that everything - the earth beneath me, the sky above, the plant life that surrounded me - had a very distinct sensation to it, like being close enough to a wood stove to sense its heat without being close enough for it to truly warm you.

Over the years, I realized that this was the first part of the lesson. The exercise had been specifically designed to teach me to open my eyes and see the world around me as alive and vibrant, not just as the backdrop for my busy life. Each night the world opened a little more to me. Some days it seemed as if the trees whispered wordlessly to each other, just beyond the reach of my hearing. When the weekend came, I sat in the sun, watching the sparrows trace patterns in the sky. It wasn't so much that each thing I saw had a lesson to teach me - I wasn't far enough along on my path to realize that yet - it was that my perception began to slowly change, that I began to see the world around me as being alive. And, because it was truly alive to me, each thing I saw had an intrinsic value. As a part of that weave of life, as an integral part of the world around me, I realized that my life had value too, and over the years I would learn to see the special gift that each of us holds that makes us magickal and unique.

OOO

Decades ago, I participated in a spiritual discussion group where we considered a series of books that were channeled from a spirit known as White Eagle. The class was led by a very gentle soul who had that twinkle in his eye, the one that suggests he knew just a little more than he let on. It was that feeling you get from a teacher when they supply you with a line of bread crumbs and allow you to follow it in your own way and in your own time. His name was Gary and he gave us a single guideline to follow at the very beginning of our first class.

"This is channeled material," he began. "You can't simply take it at face value. What you have to remember is that each and every one of us has our own prejudices and our own experiences that we filter such information through. The author of this book was not immune to that, no matter how much we would like to pretend otherwise. We can't blindly accept these words as the author presents them. Instead, we have to do our best to understand the author's perspective and remove the author's fingerprints from the words before us."

Of all of the instruction that I've been offered over the years, this small morsel has been more consistently useful to me than any other. Any sort of spiritual insight - whether it's a recognized holy text, channeled material, or information gleaned from our own interaction with the spirit world - cannot be accepted wholly at face value. We have to remove the taint of the perspective and prejudice that the material was filtered through. This concept has applications, not just when approaching channeled material, but in accepting instruction from any teacher (incarnated or otherwise), when engaging in meditative or shamanic journeying, or simply gleaning information from the energetic landscape around us.

The key behind this concept is pretty simple. To access material from the Elsewhere, whether we're contacting an entity or embarking on a shamanic journey, we have to achieve a certain state of consciousness, similar in many ways to how we experience the Dreamtime. In this state, symbolism becomes a critical component of the communication between our conscious mind, our subconscious, our spirit, and the spirit world. We're working on Level Two and symbolism is the language of that realm. Our conscious mind often takes a passive role in journeying, becoming an observer and a recorder. It's our spirit that leads the way, teaming with our subconscious mind to paint the landscape we experience.

You can think of opening to this type of information in a manner similar to riding a wild horse. Our conscious mind is little more than a video camera, capturing the experience for playback at a later date. For the most part, it is not in control of the experience. In fact, if we engage our conscious mind to too great of an extent, it tends to ground us and pull us out of the journey.

Imagine that you're on the back of a spirited, nearly unbroken stallion, trying to ride toward a specific destination or attempting to study or observe something on the path right in front of you. We can visualize that we're hanging onto the neck of a rearing, skittering horse for dear life, that as it abruptly changes direction the landscape before us changes with its course. But that's not quite right. A much more accurate perspective would be that our steed, a poorly understood merging of our spirit and subconscious, actually changes the symbolism of everything that we interact with.

For example, let's imagine that you had an encounter with a vicious canine somewhere in your childhood. Not only did the creature bite you, but ever since you've harbored a deeply rooted fear of dogs.

In the midst of your journeying, you're approached by Wolf, a spirit often associated with teaching energy. However, because your subconscious has such a prominent role in journeying and you have previously established feelings where dogs are concerned, one of two things will generally happen. Either your subconscious mind masks the form of Wolf, creating new symbolism (perhaps turning Wolf into an old wise woman or even another animal) and you risk losing the full meaning behind the encounter - or your fears manifest and Wolf is seen as a huge, menacing creature and the entire message is heavily influenced by your prejudices where canines are concerned.

This is an obvious example of how this process works. But imagine that you enter the encounter with a strong opinion on how the Divine manifests. Or that you believe in a battle between darkness and light and everything must be framed as either a threat or an ally. Perhaps you have very low self-esteem and a nurturing and compassionate manifestation of the Goddess is turned demanding and emotionally distant by your subconscious mind. Imagine that, through the exercise above, you learn to open yourself to the energy all around us but already have strong ideas regarding how a situation you're involved in should play out. In any of those situations, unless you are aware of your filters and willing to set aside your ego to move beyond them, the information that you "retrieve" will be highly slanted based upon your own prejudices and will lack any sort of reliable accuracy.

When I work with students, I spend a great deal of time focusing on spiritual growth and the importance of learning to let go of fear and fully embracing love. There are a handful of key reasons to do so, reasons that immediately and concretely impact our ability to work magick and interact with the spirit realm. With a typical student, the first mystical benefit that is gained by embracing this process is the ability to see clearly.

This is a lesson that I learned firsthand and one that I still strive to promote in my own practice. Before I am anything else, I am a simple student myself. There is always something more to learn, some other challenge to overcome, another shadow to let go and allow love to fill that once darkened space. From time to time, I still find my own prejudices influencing a journey and, when I re-center and let them go, I have literally watched the entire landscape of the journey change before my eyes.

There is a concept that comes into play in our own spiritual growth. At its heart is the simple principle that the more we learn and grow, the more opportunity we're given. What begins as a process of learning to clearly see the energetic landscape around us, becomes a process of accepting the full potential of spiritual reality. And accepting that on one level of reality will open up doors on other levels of reality.

In late 1998, I was collecting sea salt for use in ritual work on a secluded beach outside of San Francisco when I found myself being shadowed by a spirit. I stopped and addressed it and the spirit introduced herself to me, offering to teach me what secrets she knew and aid in my spiritual growth. What's more is that she gave me a name to use whenever I chose to call her to my side. In the lore of our family, she became known as "the goddess of the sea," and I called upon her and worked with her on numerous occasions.

Several years later, having grown a considerable amount and having reached the point where I'd let go of many of my own prejudices, I called upon "the goddess of the sea" while doing some shamanic work on the Oregon Coast. I had no preconceived ideas of how the encounter would unfold, but was simply open to whatever work we might do together that day as I'd been receiving lessons from her for some time.

"I am not the goddess of the sea, but her handmaiden," she said in her language that wasn't a language. (The word "handmaiden" wasn't exactly right, but I've never found a term that fits better than that.) "Would you like to meet the one that I serve?"

I was given a name to use when calling upon this goddess, its form ancient and sing-song, not a single name but one layered in three parts, almost like a primitive poem. As I stood there on the shoreline, I uttered the threefold name, not knowing what to expect and doing my best to simply be open to whatever might happen. The "goddess" materialized, not in the surf before me, but upon the horizon, "her" form dominating the expanse of ocean that lay before my eyes. She was ancient. Primal. Elemental. There was no need to anthropomorphize her, to try to fit her into human form, because there was nothing even remotely human about her. To put it simply, she was awe-inspiring.

That encounter not only enabled me to let go of more of my preconceived ideas, but opened other doors for me. No longer did I need a deity to fit into a simple human-shaped form. I was now aware that there were spiritual beings that held an indescribable level of power, a concept that reshaped my own understanding of the spirits that we could interact with on our path. And that's how magick works. Each step forward on our path presents us with new landscapes, with new challenges, and opens us to experiences (and please consider both the irony and truth of the latter part of this statement) that we never believed possible.

At first glance, letting go of our prejudices and preconceived ideas may seem like a daunting task - even more so when we attempt to apply it to words, wisdom, or insight channeled through another's psyche or gleaned from the energetic landscape around us. The good news is that we already have the necessary framework in place to do the work.

First, we need an ethical structure to guide us, such as the spiritual paths we already embrace. Rather than replacing one set of preconceived ideas with a new set of the same, a series of ethical guidelines and standards provide us with a mirror to gaze into, something in which we find our challenges reflected. By striving to become more than we are, we slowly begin to let go of those things that prevent us from seeing clearly.

Second, we need a detection system in place, something that will notify us when we are filtering the information we receive. Thankfully, we already have that too. Whenever we have an emotional response to an experience, regardless of whether we label that emotion as positive or negative, we're filtering what is present in that moment. We can often look at emotion as an internal warning system. All we have to do is notice that we're having an emotional response, step back and ask ourselves, "Why do I feel this way?"

When we find the source, whether it's a fear, an insecurity, or a wound that we suffered along the way, all we have to do is heal the wound - and the easiest way to do so is to forgive those involved, including ourselves, and learn to love those involved in the situation. By learning to love, we disarm the prejudice and let it go. And with the prejudice out of the way, we can see clearly and our path continues to open up before us. Likewise, rather than finding a wound, we may discover that it's a hope, dream, or wish that has suddenly come to life before our eyes. Then the moment becomes one where we can express gratitude and thankfulness, both of which are keys that unlock ever-deeper portions of the spiritual landscape.

Even when we work with secondhand materials, we need to look for patterns and measure them against an ethical framework. The easiest rule of thumb is to look at it in the light of the core of the Divine - perfect Love. The absence of love creates fear. Fear creates limitations. Limitations create boundaries. We slowly see where an author begins to say, "You must do this" or "You cannot do that" and realize that they are placing restrictions on the Divine. Each path, each voice, contains a bit of truth, a tiny fragment of the whole. These voices overlap in a chorus, not where they draw lines, but where they are allowed the freedom to merge and flow.

It's in these places where we can begin to gain a glimpse of the sacred - and using that glimpse as a mirror, we can slowly whittle away at our own prejudices and preconceived ideas and begin to see more clearly.

CHAPTER FIVE

THE MOST IMPORTANT LAW IN MAGICK

Most of us, at one point or another, have encountered modern Christianity. Whether it was in the form of a Christian neighbor, a childhood spent in Sunday School, or a time when our path called the Church home, we typically hold at least a cursory familiarity with that path.

One of my favorite verses that has magickal applications is Matthew 18:18. (Surprised to find reference to a Bible verse in a book on magick? Don't be. If magick is real, you'll find bits and pieces of it everywhere you look; if it's not real, it will be completely absent from other paths.) The NIV translation of that verse has Jesus telling us, "Truly I tell you, whatever you bind on earth will be bound in heaven, and whatever you loose on earth will be loosed in heaven."

This is simply another way of stating what practitioners have known from a time long before these words were spoken. It's also a perspective that is sometimes easier for new students to embrace that the more occult phrasing of the same concept.

See, there's a mystical rule of thumb that is most commonly referenced from a work known as *The Emerald*

Tablet of Hermes Trismegistus. I imagine that there are many of you who are asking, "Who in the heck is Hermes Trismegistus? And does *The Emerald Tablet* have anything to do with The Emerald City from the Wizard of Oz?"

Hermes Trismegistus is an ancient deity (somewhere between 323 BCE and 146 BCE) where the people of the time took the Greek god Hermes and squished him together with the Egyptian god Thoth. For a time, the two gods were worshiped as one in the Temple of Thoth in Khmu (Egypt), which the Greeks referred to as Hermopolis.

No one is absolutely certain when *The Emerald Tablet* was written or who wrote it. However, given its formal name, it is connected to a divine source (though unlikely in a literal sense.) What we do know for certain is that *The Emerald Tablet* has been held in the highest regard for countless centuries by occultists and is the foundation of European alchemy. The translation that I prefer (the earliest text of *The Emerald Tablet* is in Arabic) was written by a French master alchemist who went by the pseudonym of Fulcanelli. No one knows exactly who this person was as he published several works in the early 1900s under his *nom de plume* and then subsequently disappeared without a trace.

It is easiest to think of *The Emerald Tablet* as the mystical equivalent of the laws of physics. If you set a spoon so that it is hanging half-way off the edge of a table and give the exposed portion a good whack, physics will detail the angle, speed, and distance that spoon will fly. If you're walking a mystical path and intending to do magick, *The Emerald Tablet* will go a long way toward explaining how and why your workings will succeed or fail.

The Fulcanelli translation reads as follows:

1.   This is the truth, the whole truth and nothing but the truth:

2.   As below, so above; and as above so below. With this knowledge alone you may work miracles.

3.   And since all things exist in and emanate from the ONE Who is the ultimate Cause, so all things are born after their kind from this ONE.

4. The Sun is the father, the Moon the mother; the wind carried it in his belly. Earth is its nurse and its guardian.

5. It is the Father of all things,

6. The eternal Will is contained in it.

7. Here, on earth, its strength, its power remain one and undivided. Earth must be separated from fire, the subtle from the dense, gently with unremitting care.

8. It arises from the earth and descends from heaven; it gathers to itself the strength of things above and things below.

9. By means of this one thing all the glory of the world shall be yours and all obscurity flee from you.

10. It is power, strong with the strength of all power, for it will penetrate all mysteries and dispel all ignorance. By it the world was created.

11. From it are born manifold wonders, the means to achieving which are here given

12. It is for this reason that I am called Hermes Trismegistus; for I possess the three essentials of the philosophy of the universe.

13. This is the sum total of the work of the Sun.

The Emerald Tablet clearly speaks of the application and flow of magick although it does so in a hidden, symbolic manner. This is the traditional approach to sharing knowledge where magick is concerned. (In case you haven't noticed, I'm something of a rebel and prefer to share things in a way that they're at least somewhat easy to understand.)

Some of the text of *The Emerald Tablet* may seem familiar to you. Have you ever watched a legal drama on television? Then you've probably heard the first line countless times. "... The truth, the whole truth and nothing but the truth." This phrase has been used since the Middle Ages in legal proceedings and while no one knows exactly where the phrase came from, magick used to be taken seriously by the masses. Go back in time a few centuries and magick was not only a serious practice, but believed to be real by the vast percentage of the populace. Famous Western occultists include Ptolemy, Roger Bacon, Pope John XXII, Heinrich Cornelius Agrippa, Nostradamus, Sir Walter Raleigh, Sir Isaac Newton, William Blake, Sir Arthur Conan Doyle, William Butler Yeats, and countless others. While I'm not suggesting that the Western legal system swiped this line of text from The *Emerald Tablet*, I will suggest that the phrase was important enough that both our legal system and *The Emerald Tablet* were inspired from the same source.

The second line reads simply, " As below, so above; and as above so below. With this knowledge alone you may work miracles." Let's think about the latter half of that phrase for a moment. "With this knowledge alone you may work miracles." Isn't that what we're attempting to do in magick? Isn't that what Jesus was renowned for during his time?

Look at the similarities between the two phrases: "... whatever you bind on earth will be bound in heaven, and whatever you loose on earth will be loosed in heaven" and "As below, so above; and as above so below." A symmetry between physical and spiritual reality is described in both phrases; not just as a mirror, but a principle that actions on one plane will have results on the other. Regardless of which direction that you choose to approach the concept - from your mundane mindset and actions influencing the spiritual weave around you or using spiritual means (such as spellwork) to influence mundane reality, this phrase is a clear key to the working of magick.

After all, once you're removed all of the dogma, what's the real difference between a Christian's miracle and a practitioner's magick?

The concept of "As below, so above," (or ABSA, as I like to call it) is simple to embrace at first glance, but the applications and secrets that it reveals are nearly endless. At its heart is the principle that physical and spiritual reality are not only connected, but that they mirror each other. We've considered the fact that we're all Spirit, that All is One, that we are spiritual beings who have chosen to experience reality from a physical perspective, but ABSA is our first key that begins to unlock what all of that means.

While my students are generally pretty amazing individuals, occasionally you can feel this subconscious rolling of the eyes when I talk about spiritual growth and interpersonal relationships.   After all, didn't they seek me out to learn magick? But if ABSA is real, then how we interact with the spirits who have incarnated with us will also influence how we interact with the spirits we seek to interact with in our magick. If spiritual growth removes the mundane limitations that we've put in place that limit our perceived access to Spirit, how can focusing on our spiritual growth do anything other than significantly increase the magickal power at our fingertips?

And this is just the tip of the proverbial iceberg where ABSA is concerned.

The concept of "As below, so above," gives us a template for crafting our ritual. Why do we use Elements in our magickal workings? Because those same Elements are the building blocks of reality so it makes sense to use them as the building blocks of our ritual when we're seeking to change or replace a specific piece of that same reality. What item or concept do we choose to represent Earth when working a protection spell? What about an iron nail, to hammer the protection into place and close harmful access to our target? What about a metal padlock to do the same? Or a key? Or a wooden dollhouse door?

What we seek to accomplish when crafting a ritual is to take the energetic building blocks for the working and assemble them in such a manner that we create a symbolic mirror of our intent. The more accurate that mirror, the more accurate the working. "As below, so above." We raise energy to empower the rite to move our intent from symbolism to an energetic package that we entrust to the spirit world. The more energy we raise, the more successfully we bridge the gap between the realms of the mundane and spiritual; the better our relationship with the people in our world, the better our relationship with the spirits that we work with in our rite. This is the foundation of successful magick.

The actual working that we do is somewhat irrelevant. It isn't important that the ritual or spell that you work was written by the Grand Poo-Bah of the Mystic Lodge of the Cosmic Lucky Rabbit's Foot. Think of your working not as a test where you have to get enough of the answers right that you achieve a passing grade, but as writing an energetic letter. What's important is that you capture the meaning and intent behind your rite and empower it with energy. A desperate eleventh hour prayer has as much or more "oomph" behind it as the most carefully prepared spell, practiced under the full moon on sacred ground at midnight on October 31st.

See, sometimes magick can take the form of a letter (a ritual) and sometimes it's a verbal plea (a prayer). Both are equally effective. You don't ever need to do something a certain way because someone else told you to do so; you need to learn to do it your way in a manner that feels "right" to you and resonates with your core. Trust your intuition; follow your heart. They won't lead you astray.

The principle embodied in "As below, so above" is critical to the very existence of magick. ABSA bridges two key levels of reality that we looked at earlier: Level Two (where symbolism becomes the language of magick) and Level Three (where miracles take place). It empowers and enables us to step beyond the rigid framework of the physical realm and interact with the fabric of reality. It is not only the conduit through which magick flows but the thread that holds the seams of "All is One" together in a unified whole.

When we think of working magick, we often think of ourselves in a physical place, moving physical objects an altar or circle in a manner that reflects our intent for the rite. It would be more accurate to suggest that a magickal working is one where we are detached from the situation and putting players in place to influence the outcome of the situation. (It would be even more accurate to speak of multidimensional reality, non-linear time, and the synthesis of uniting our energetic bodies in a working, but the following will get the basic idea across to you.)

Imagine that you have a team of professional actors at your disposal and a budget of several thousand dollars. The same patron who provided you with money and manpower has tasked you with improving the life of one specific person, a cashier at a local bookstore, over the course of a single day. The catch is that you can't directly engage with your target or anyone that may be a part of their world in a manner that would hire them to carry out a role or somehow bring them into your "hidden play." Everything has to be done behind the scenes.

You make your plans around a table in your living room, assigning the roles to the various thespians and having a personal assistant acquire the props that you'll need. Working late into the evening, you finally have your course of action in place and agree that the plan will be executed the next morning.

As your target leaves their apartment on their way to work and crosses the sidewalk, an attractive person of the opposite sex smiles and offers them a friendly and unanticipated, "Good morning." Late for the bus, they yell at the driver who is beginning to pull away, only to have a stranger (another actor) catch the driver's attention, step in front of the bus, and hold it long enough for your target to make the commute. A street musician plays their favorite song a few blocks from their work, customers ask for recommendations and express their thanks and gratitude to both the bookstore cashier and (in one case) the cashier's manager, and around lunchtime a pizza is delivered (an apparent prank as it names a non-existent employee) and the delivery person says with a smile, "You might as well keep it - we'll just throw it out anyway." Near the end of the cashier's shift, a French tourist (another actor) appears to purchase a travel guide, and because of our target's good mood and extra helpfulness due to pleasant and appreciative customers, the tourist invites our cashier to accompany them on the town, all expenses paid.

The cashier's day ends with a free lunch, a free night on the town, massive amounts of good energy, their boss seeing them in a favorable light - and those are just the pieces directly related to your efforts. Is the cashier, who was beginning to withdraw from their social circle, now more likely to call and connect with their friend? Does the co-worker or customer who had a small crush on the cashier suddenly ask them out after watching them being so helpful and in demand? Will the bus driver look twice the next day to make sure our cashier isn't running late? Does the high powered business person in line behind one of the customers our cashier helped return the next day to offer our target a much better paying job?

"As below, so above" allows all of that to happen *even if we never leave our table where we planned the day's events.* When we sat down with the actors and our assistant, we put certain energies in play that were carried out without our direct intervention. When we work a rite, our "assistants" are the Elements, the sun and the moon, the time of day, the symbolism we instilled in the rite, and our "budget" is the relationship we've built with the spirit realm and the Divine, primarily through the way we live our life and treat the people in our world.

When applied to magickal work, ABSA isn't tremendously more complex than that. There is no guarantee that our cashier will even hear the friendly, "Good morning." The bus can honk at the delaying actor and keep driving. The manager of the bookstore may have strong opinions of our cashier that a mountain of positive customer feedback will never change. Perhaps our cashier is tired and turns down the French tourist's invitation. Maybe the pizza is declined.

See, if "All is One" then everything is likewise Spirit. This means that, from a shaman's perspective, everything is alive. This also means that each and every thing in all of reality has its own journey. We can't magickally keep the Thanksgiving turkey from decaying, simply because we would be derailing the turkey's journey, the journey of the meat itself, and the journey of the bacteria and microbes that will be drawn to the carcass. The turkey isn't destined to remain forever fresh in our refrigerator; it is destined, like all life, to return to the soil and continue the cycle of life, death, and rebirth. What's more is that you have your own journey, which is why spiritual growth and personal evolution is so critical to a magick practice. If you are seriously out of sync with your own spirit and your own path, it becomes tremendously difficult to influence the events around you until you reestablish that balance.

Nothing, including magick, will ever be a foolproof solution to the challenges you face. It isn't a sure thing, but it is a method of influencing the events in your world within a healthy and appropriate framework. That doesn't mean that magick doesn't work. What it does mean is that magick works in its own way and on a timetable that is typically slower than what we've come to expect from the flow of our modern world.

The rest of The Emerald Tablet? You're not ready for it. That's not a slight or an insult, it is simply a way of saying, "Your magickal practice will naturally unfold." You can stay up late for thousands of nights in a row, studying each and every phrase and they won't open to you. That's not how magick works. But if you live your life to the fullest, if you focus on your growth, the relationships in your world, and become the best "you" that you can be, don't be surprised if you glance at The Emerald Tablet every so often and suddenly a new section begins to make sense to you. Just as you can't pry open your life to instantly change it, neither can you simply demand the secrets in magick and have them fall into your hands. It isn't an equation; it's a journey that you walk one step at a time. Remember, "As below, so above." Each step on your path not only influences the moments in your waking world, it simultaneously changes your access to the spirit world as well. We're Spirit, each and every one of us. The more completely that begins to resonate with you, the easier and more powerfully your magick will flow.

CHAPTER SIX

A SPIRITUAL ECOSYSTEM

The full phrase that I refer to as ABSA states, "As below, so above; and as above so below. With this knowledge alone you may work miracles." Drawn from a text known as The Emerald Tablet, this principle is a reminder - not only that all things are connected and interrelated, but that everything that exists within our lives is echoed on different levels of reality. Sometimes we may find these echoes in dreams, appearing as visions that give us insight into our daily lives. These echoes permeate the natural world, the weave of nature acting like a mirror in which we can learn to see ourselves. And at times, we can even find these echoes in each other.

This concept is one of the cornerstones of magick. Simply put, anything that falls outside of this principle will not work as intended. On the rare occasions that a magickal working outside of "As below, so above" (ABSA) is successful, it's simply because we're not seeing the entire energetic template that is framing the situation. Rather than a hard and fast law that reality holds to, ABSA is a key that unlocks reality. It doesn't say, "Things must be this way," but rather, "This is how to see beyond the illusion of the merely physical to the spiritual nature of reality."

Even if you had no other tool than ABSA to work with, you would be successful in unraveling the secrets of magick. ABSA places a mirror in our hands in which we can see how physical reality is a reflection of the spirit realm. Want to deepen your connection with spirits? First deepen your connection with the people in your life. Want to gain additional power? Discover how to gain real, unshakable power within yourself and embrace who you truly are at your core. Magick isn't a process of being measured and found ready before you can take the next step into the mysteries; it's a journey where the more we embrace Spirit, the more clearly we see the true nature of reality.

Imagine that you're standing in the midst of an ancient library, but your eyes are wrapped in heavy gauze. The first step is not in assuming that there is a nearly forgotten language that you need to learn to access the material, but in removing the bandages from your eyes so you can see.

At each milepost along the path, we find this same lesson. The door before us is never about finding a key or breaking the barrier down, but in releasing our need to find a way through the portal. When we let go of our preconceived ideas and limitations, the door doesn't simply disappear; we suddenly find ourselves standing in the room beyond the barrier. The tools we hold are then applied to the material we find within the chamber, until we've worked our way to the next door.

This process doesn't simply repeat itself, but our successes build, one upon the other. We begin finding open corridors where once there were closed doors. The process of letting go begins to saturate throughout our being and we find that, as the lessons become a part of us, they are instantly and intuitively applied to countless challenges before us on our path.

In one of the countless brilliant bits of synchronicity along our journey, we find ourselves immersed in the very fabric of ABSA everywhere we turn. If physical reality is truly a manifestation of spiritual energy, then both the people in our lives and the natural world around us are filled to overflowing with countless lessons and insights that are simply waiting for us to discover them.

When we embark on a spiritual path, we are much like an acorn that is beginning the journey to becoming a mighty oak. Around us are all the things we need to thrive and grow. For the fledgling oak tree, these resources would manifest themselves as nutrient-rich soil, the gentle rain, and the life-giving, guiding light of the sun. As the newly born tree begins to reach for the sun, it will face tests and trials. There will be storms to weather, droughts to survive, and parasites to withstand. But each year that passes, the tree will add another ring to its trunk; it will grow a little stronger, a little taller. With its new-found strength it finds that the storms that once threatened its very existence are much easier to withstand. As it nears the light of the sun that it reaches for, its perspective begins to change. Where it once lived in a world of darkness beneath the soil, the tiny sapling broke through into the light of the world. As it continued to grow, it left behind an existence where life was a wall of grass and low shrubs, until it towered above the forest and could see to the horizon.

We are very similar to the acorn. Around us, we have all the resources we need to grow, and life is quick to throw challenges our way. Each of us has our sun to reach for, a journey where our heart is our map and our intuition our compass. For some of us, we are on a quest for wisdom and enlightenment. For others, we may simply be seeking to add value to our lives. Whatever our quest is, we reach for the sun, believing that it is right for us to leave the sheltering darkness of the soil to break into the light of the world above.

But before we can grow, we must awaken to the world around us. An acorn cannot make the transition from seed to sapling without first experiencing the soil that shelters it; it must be able to sense the sun before it can reach for its light. Likewise, we cannot make the transition from dreamer to seeker without reaching beyond our shells. Dreamers are content to wonder what lays beyond them, to imagine what they could achieve if they took the steps to grow. Seekers believe their dreams are a roadmap, a glimpse of the path ahead, and they dare to take the steps that will lead them to the place where their dreams are alive.

.he physical realm is truly a mirror of spiritual reality,
ve connect to the natural energy that surrounds us?
we reach beyond our shells to experience the world?

Whether we live in the middle of a city or in the depths
of the wilderness, there are two sources of natural energy we
can draw upon. The first is the sky. Wherever we live, the
sun shines upon us and the moon travels across the heavens
at night. The second source is the natural energy around us,
whether it is a forest, the ocean, a city park, or even a tree that
grows on an urban street.

Connecting with the sun is the easiest method to
connect with natural energy and one of the simplest steps
we'll take on this path. Each morning, go to a place where you
can face the east, the direction the sun rises. Take a moment
to notice the sunrise or the early morning sun (if you don't
get up early enough to catch the transition from night to day).
Stand in front of your window (or outside, if your living
situation allows it) and simply experience the sunlight. Take
a moment and watch how the light looks different on the
world around you than it does in the afternoon. If you're up
early enough to watch the sunrise, pay attention to the colors,
to the different hues that are painted across the clouds. No
two sunrises are the same. Each morning, you'll be blessed
with a special moment alone with nature's majesty.

As you stand there, experiencing the morning
sunlight, take a moment to welcome the sun. This could be
something as simple as saying, "Sun, I welcome you to a new
day," or as elaborate as reciting a poem that you wrote about
the sunrise. It doesn't matter if you speak the words aloud or
simply think them in your mind. What is important is that
you take a moment to specifically welcome the sun into your
day.

Why? Each moment of our life is sacred. Think
about it for a moment. Is there any object in your world that
is more important to you than your life? While many of us
would readily lay down our lives for those we love, that's
our choice. But what if someone was ready to take away all
your choices? What price would you accept to have all your
choices taken away, to have someone else completely control
your will? You would not be allowed to disobey, to resist,
but would have to contently serve their every need as their

slave, not their servant, until the end of time. Not one of us would do that. Why? Because our lives are important to us. Whether we have trouble admitting it or not, our lives have value. We are each filled with the sacred spark of life. Each of us is a unique expression of the entire expanse of reality. Rather than simply being physical beings, we are love, dreams, imagination, and emotion wrapped in a physical package. We are life. And each of us is extremely sacred for that reason.

Yet we race through life at a breakneck pace, almost as if we seek to move so quickly that we miss the quiet moments around us. We jump out of bed with our alarm clock and click on the television to fill our morning. We race to the car, turning up the radio for the drive to work. Each moment we surround ourselves with distractions, things that keep our mind occupied as moments pass into days and days into years. In the midst of it all, the sun rises each morning, the moon slowly goes through its cycle, and the seasons slowly turn.

And we are oblivious to it all.

As we take a moment each morning to welcome the sun, we stop the maelstrom around us. We pause to recognize the sacred. Rather than distracting ourselves from life, we take a moment to embrace it. Where we were once separate from the cycles of nature that are all around us, we begin to become a part of them. As we stand there, our eyes closed, welcoming the sun to a new day, we become a part of that sunrise. We make ourselves a part of that cycle, and in doing so, we begin to reconnect ourselves to the weave of nature that surrounds us.

This simple daily practice gives you a reference to understand the cycles of your day. By taking a few moments to honor the day and the night, you begin to bring order to your day. Your subconscious mind, instead of running around tired all day, coming home and vegetating in front of the television, and suddenly being thrust into bed, now has a regular division to its day. You'll find that your stress level should slowly and naturally drop, that you become more focused on the tasks before you, and that you have more energy to complete them with.

The second reason this exercise is important is because it begins to connect you to the larger cycles of the natural world. The moon and sun each have very distinct cycles, both physically and on an energetic level. Rather than being pulled by these cycles, you'll notice them and find that your own energies begin to synchronize with them. When was the last time you instinctively knew when the moon was new? When was the last time that you thought, "You know, the flowers should be blooming any day now," simply because you somehow intuitively knew it was time for them to do so? Both the sun and moon have a multitude of subtle influences on our lives. We may get cranky when the hours of daylight start to shorten or feel energized on the full moon. Rather than simply stumbling into these patterns, by regularly observing them we begin to understand them and make them a part of our lives.

The third reason we do this exercise is simply to begin changing our frame of mind. The path I teach isn't one where we expect to grow simply because we deserve it. Rather, we begin to seek our natural place in the world, working with the rhythms of life rather than fighting against them.

One of the most important magickal phrases we'll learn to use is composed of two simple words: "Thank you." That compact phrase has applications in everything from spiritual growth to empowering magick.

Saying, "Thank you," in a rite is an act of manifestation. We don't give thanks when something we ask for doesn't come through; we say thank you when after it has happened. By giving thanks as part of our rite, we're stating, "This shall come to pass."

Saying, "Thank you," builds a connection between ourselves and the spirit world. We give thanks for a gift that is given and express our appreciation to the giver. If we are the recipient of the gift (the intent of our rite) then the spirit world is the one who gives us that gift. By saying, "Thank you," we build a connection of generosity and thankfulness between us and the spirit world. That connection alone opens all kinds of useful doors for us.

Saying, "Thank you" - and meaning it - opens up our energetic centers. Our energy shifts, sometimes radically, when we express our thankfulness. Giving thanks is one of the easiest ways to lower our walls and open up our energy to an experience.

Saying, "Thank you," keeps us centered and balanced. It's very easy to lose sight of where we should be on our paths. Sometimes we will simply thank the world around us for a blessed experience. Occasionally, we will simply stop and thank ourselves for taking the steps to reach a certain point in our personal growth.

To properly understand this material, you must move beyond the mindset that we're separate from the natural cycles around us. By giving thanks, we instinctively assume that we are receiving something from nature - which we are. By looking at our lives as receiving a multitude of blessings, we begin to understand that we aren't taking from the world, but that we are equals in the great cycle of life.

Ego says, "That's not true. Mankind was given this world to shape and submit to our will. We are, without question, the King of the Hill." I disagree. Try living without sunlight or oxygen. Try living without water. The rivers, the trees, the sky, and the sun can continue on without us, but we cannot continue on without them. Begin to say, "Thank you," on a regular basis and you will slowly begin to understand the inherent blessings and joy found in simply being alive. As we begin to understand that we are in an equal partnership with life, instead of simply subduing it to our will, we begin to perceive that we are part of a larger, interconnected web of existence. This might not seem important now, but there are secrets that will unfold for you if you apply ABSA to the situation.

There's an ancient belief that magickal practitioners don't find their power by commanding nature; those that truly find the magick on this path do so by developing a partnership, a relationship, and a friendship with the natural world around them. By welcoming the day and night on a regular basis, you can begin to embrace this perspective now - which will benefit you greatly, not only today, but as your studies and your path continue to unfold.

CHAPTER SEVEN

BRIDGING THE GAP

When I begin working with a student, regardless of whether they're an experienced practitioner or they're spreading their spiritual wings for the very first time, one of the first things we do is test their boundaries. In physical endeavors, such as coaching my children in one of their little league sports, you test boundaries by determining what a person can do. How well do they throw and catch a ball? Can they dribble a basketball and shoot a basket? How is their swing from the plate and can they consistently hit a baseball?

Abilities such as these are one of the methods we employ to measure the world around us. For instance, I know that I can throw a ball a certain distance or I can hit a baseball with a bat when the pitch is thrown below a certain speed and over a specific part of the plate. Measuring these abilities in a young athlete gives me an idea of their strengths and weaknesses, indicating where we need to focus our work and where I can offer sincere praise.

Spirituality, even that which is integrated into a mystical path where we learn skills like ritual and spellwork, requires a different approach. It's not important to me how deep of a trance state a student can reach or how well they can raise, move, and ground energy. Each of us has talents and abilities that are unique to us as individuals and I don't believe that there is a certain skill set necessary to becoming a practitioner or being able to work magick. What I'm looking for when I work with a student are the boundaries that say, "My universe exists this far, but no farther" or "I believe I'm capable of achieving this mystical result, but not that one."

Almost without exception, our first lesson together is designed to tear those boundaries down. It's not a clean process; not a situation where you can push a button, the student's walls disappear, and they're left standing in awe as they look in wonder at the vastness of reality. But I can stretch out my hand and offer them a seed. It's up to each student whether they take that seed and what they do with it. Some will politely accept it and toss it aside as the ravings of a slightly unbalanced shaman. Some will tuck it away in a drawer or a back pocket, meaning to consider it later, but quickly forgetting that they were offered a seed at all. It's actually quite rare that a student will take the seed, plant it in soil, and carefully nurture it. There is no telling what the seed will grow into. Each harvest is as unique as the person who reaps it. But they will find a harvest. Perhaps it will manifest as a single flower. Perhaps it will become an apple tree ripe with fruit. But those who plant the seed will find the path before them and, their eyes open, will have the opportunity to see that path stretching to the horizon.

The seed that I offer them looks something like this.

"We know absolutely nothing - and we know everything." You'll hear spiritual teachers utter phrases like that all the time without explaining what they mean. While they mean well, intending for the student to discover the meaning of the statement for themselves on the path to enlightenment, well, I'm enough of a spiritual rebel that I prefer to hand out the teacher's edition of the books and like to offer the reasons behind the answers.

We know that we experience life. At this point in the process, it doesn't matter whether you're a fan of reincarnation or an adherent to the "we only live one lifetime" philosophy. (By the way, both are true; spiritual reality is incredibly diverse.) All that's truly important is that we can agree on that single point, that we experience life. (If you're having trouble coming to terms with the concept, pinch yourself. Feel that? Then you're experiencing life. It's really that simple.) Understanding that we experience life is our first milepost on this particular journey.

The second milepost is that our experiences tend to fall into one of two categories - things we enjoy and things that we don't. Unless you've been seriously wounded at some point in your journey, to the point where there is a need for some deep healing to take place, you will find yourself drawn toward experiences that are pleasant rather than those that are unpleasant. The very act of experiencing, of dividing experiences into categories, is a process of learning. We learn that eating chocolate is a pleasant experience, one we'd like to repeat – and that biting our tongue hard enough to draw blood is an experience we'd like to avoid. In the same manner, we learn that comfort is pleasant and fear is unpleasant; that compassion is pleasant and rejection unpleasant; that love is pleasant and that hate is unpleasant. And, as we've considered at numerous points on our journey together, at its heart, spirituality is about love.

To truly experience love, we must first learn to love ourselves - and that can take some work. Perhaps we've eaten too much chocolate and don't like our reflection or the size of our clothes. Maybe we weren't given enough chocolate as a child and feel unworthy to receive it when it's offered to us as adults. We learn to heal, learn to forgive, and ultimately, learn to love. These are lessons that not only draw us closer to a life we find as pleasant (as opposed to unpleasant) but are lessons that are universally lauded by those we recognize as holy men and women.

So now we know two things. First of all, we're here to experience life. Second, those experiences, led by nothing more than our choice of experiencing the pleasant qualities of life, ultimately lead us to a spiritual path. One of the first boundaries that we have to let go of is usually found right here. Students will chime in with the observation that not everyone adopts a religion or even a defined faith. And those students are absolutely right. However, it isn't the definition of a path that makes it spiritual, it's what's in a person's heart. You don't have to consider yourself Christian or Muslim or Wiccan or a follower of any path to be on one. It's what you feel, how you've learned to respond rather than react, and how you put your own needs aside to honor a loved one's needs that defines a spiritual path.

The mother who holds a screaming child in her arms, rocking the infant back and forth, gently cooing words of love and comfort until the baby quiets down? She's the same woman who couldn't stand the sound of other babies crying before she discovered the love she felt for her own infant. That's a transformative process, one where annoyance and reaction are replaced with love and response. The teacher who gives her all to her class year after year and is paid a fraction of what she could make in another career? The customer in a busy store who makes a point of smiling and offering compassion to a frazzled sales clerk? The driver who stops to help a stranded motorist change a tire in the rain? All of those people are on a spiritual path.

Labels are irrelevant. What matters is what's in your heart. This applies to absolutely everything on your path. Just be you, uniquely you, as much as you are able to be you. Every day strive to become a little more the person that you find reflected in your perspective of the Divine. Embrace your quirks, the parts of you that make you laugh and cry, the aspects of yourself that would still uniquely define you if all of our technology stopped working tomorrow. Don't worry if you read three spiritual books last month or if your daily meditation practice (well, every-other-day meditation practice) has moved up from two minutes a day to twenty. If you are truly Divine, what matters is that your heart, your core, shines through in all that you do. If you do just that, if all you do is truly embrace your unique aspect of the Divine, you're on a spiritual path. Why? Because you're taking the unique gift that Spirit created when you became an individual facet of "All is One" and you're doing your best to bring that one-of-a-kind expression of the Divine to life.

If you are a unique facet of the Divine, what happens when you bury that uniqueness beyond the templates and expectations championed by others? If you are an expression of the Divine that is found nowhere else in all of creation, what happens when you resonate the uniqueness that is you and your very core?

The third milepost takes us beyond what we can measure, but is a reflection of a concept that many of us hold up as a simple truth - the existence of an afterlife. Nearly every religion believes in a place where our soul or spirit goes or returns to after our mortal life has drawn to an end. Many of us were born into this lifetime remembering glimpses of another place, a somewhere where we existed before we came here. Young children will often speak of this place and the truth of its existence resonates in almost all of us.

For those who embrace the single lifetime model, the "Elsewhere" is somewhere to spend the remainder of eternity once this lifetime has drawn to a close. To those who believe in reincarnation, it's a place we not only came from, but where we return to between lifetimes. In both models, the "Elsewhere" is a place where we have a clearer picture of reality than we do here. Christians often believe that it's there where they'll find the answers to all of their questions. Pagans generally hold that we choose to limit what we know and remember when we incarnate into this lifetime, implying that there's a larger pool of knowledge that we have access to in the Elsewhere.

By both definitions, the Elsewhere is the dominant partner between here and there. It's there where we have access to a greater amount of information than what we readily have at our fingertips during a single incarnation. The single lifetime model believes that the Elsewhere is everlasting; after all, by that definition it's where we'll spend eternity. In reincarnation, the Elsewhere is our source and the destination of our return ticket; in other words, it's home while this lifetime is merely an extended trip.

Let's make sure that we let that concept sink in. The Elsewhere is home. Our spirits are timeless; our bodies, in a best case scenario, last no more than a century. Those of us on a magickal path tend to understand that not only is this true, but we tend to wear our mortal bodies like costumes in an epic play. Physical reality is our theater and the spirit world not only our director and crew, but the audience as well. Just like actors leaving a stage, when the curtains close on our play, we don't come to an end - we simply go home.

Being the dominant partner in the equation of reality, the Elsewhere has to be a clearer reflection of the nature of reality than what we experience in this lifetime. The source simply has "more" - more time, more knowledge, more whatever - than the product. Think of our reality as a video of a landscape and the Elsewhere being the landscape itself. One is a limited existence; the other is limited only by our imagination. If we allow ourselves to simply sit before a screen and watch the documentary of the landscape, we slowly become disconnected with who we are and what we can do. Our sphere of influence becomes the cosmic couch, the screen on which the video plays, and the remote we use to tune in and out. We forget that this is our world, that we can go outside and interact with the landscape firsthand, that we can study it, learn from it, and learn to live in harmony with it. When we strive to perceive things in this manner, we can begin to see the nature of reality slowly taking shape in the relationship between this lifetime and the place where we're referring to as the Elsewhere.

We're here to experience life. These experiences lead us to a spiritual path. Our bodies change, age, and die – and yet the essence of who we are, whether you refer to it as a soul or a spirit or something else, carries on. This spirit returns to the Elsewhere, either for eternity or for a short time before returning here. If we choose to incarnate again, we continue to grow, evolving spiritually as we continue on our spiritual path.

And it's here that the path forks. One direction leads us to consider the Elsewhere, the other to look more closely at the nature of our own mortal coil.

If we come from an Elsewhere, a place that is truly our home, and only come here to learn and spiritually evolve, then we're led to agree that the Elsewhere is a closer reflection of reality than our own mortal reality. After all, there are limitations here. We can't fly. We can't remember all of our past lives. We can't work magick.

And, given the nature of mortal reality as a reflection of the Elsewhere, there's a key reason why we can't.

Because we don't believe that we can.

If this reality is a training ground for the spirit, then, it is by its very definition, an extension of the spirit realm. We are quite literally spiritual beings who have chosen to experience life from a limited physical perspective.

What no one considers is that, if it's a choice we freely made, then we're also free to change our minds. We can remove the limitations we've agreed to accept. We can wield energy, work magick and miracles, and we can interact with the spirit world and learn from teachers who aren't currently incarnated in this mortal lifetime. If all we do is truly accept who and what we are and begin to release the boundaries that we put in place, we leave the nature of reality in this lifetime wide open.

When my eldest daughter was a toddler, we used to go on long hikes up at Opal Creek, a stretch of old growth forest with wide trails that hug the side of a mountain here in my native Oregon. My daughter would announce, "Look at that black dog!" and, five minutes later, from around the bend in a trail, would come a family with a black Labrador retriever on a leash, their party previously hidden from us by the folds of the mountain. I have pagan friends who will simply stop and focus when they need a loved one to call them - and almost without fail, the loved one will call them a short time later. I've been given visions on more than one occasion that immediately saved my son and eldest daughter from serious injury or certain death – visions that, upon reflection, I simply couldn't have pieced together from the elements in my immediate environment.

Magick works, not because we precisely follow some intricate pattern of ritual, but because we believe it will work. To be even more accurate, magick works when we stop insisting that the mystical is an impossible fantasy. A majority of the rituals, the incantations, the tools we employ not only help us focus, but they encourage us to believe. In very real ways, they act as a boost to our faith. There are rituals and tools that bridge the gap between our understanding and the result we hope to achieve, but bit by bit, as we grow comfortable with the processes and begin to understand the mystical landscape, these parts of ritual can naturally fall away. What is key is our belief.

While it is often a stretch for us to accept that this reality is simply as we define it - and that we can define it any way we choose - it's often more challenging to consider the other fork in the path. The first fork we explored led us to consider the nature of our mortal experience; the other fork invites us to consider the nature of the Elsewhere.

The question we need to consider is, if we already have a home in the Elsewhere, why would we come into this incarnation with the intention of experiencing life and growing through a process of spiritual evolution? Why would we need to grow if we'd already reached the place where we'll spend all of eternity? Why would we need to change at all if we've already succeeded in our goal?

Viewed from this perspective, there is only one answer that makes sense.

The Elsewhere isn't our final destination.

If we've already reached paradise, the afterlife, Heaven, or – as we've referred to it at this point in our journey together – the Elsewhere; if it were the end of the line, there would be no reason whatsoever for us to go through a process of growth and evolution. Evolution is a process of change, of honing traits that enable us to succeed in a particular environment. If we're leaving paradise to learn, to grow, to change into something more, then there has to be a place to apply those changes.

Some of us believe in the concept of angels or spirit guides or whatever you want to call the beings that watch over us and assist us from beyond the edge of our mortal senses. It can be argued that the reason we come here to learn and grow is to evolve into that role, to help others who choose to live this mortal lifetime. However, if this were the case, you'd eventually reach critical mass, where a Heaven filled with spirit guides would be assisting a handful of mortals who still hadn't spiritually evolved to a certain point. Mathematically, that simply doesn't work. And even if that were the case, it still raises the question, "Why become mortal at all?"

Those of us who have embraced the deeper portions of a spiritual path for a time realize that much of it isn't as much a process of collecting new spiritual tools as it is a journey of letting go. We let go of anger, we let go of fear, and ultimately, we let go of self.

There isn't one of us who, standing in the midst of a spiritual paradise, is capable of letting go of our place in that nearly perfect afterlife, knowing that we may never return and having no idea what awaits beyond that place. We don't possess the tools or perspective needed to move on to the next step in our spiritual evolution, so we come here, to the mortal experience, in order to learn how to do exactly that - let go and move on. We limit our perspective so we don't see hope, we don't see love, and we're overwhelmed with anger and fear. With the bar raised so high, we begin to learn how to let go of our self, to release our vulnerabilities in the midst of difficult situations, honing skills that will serve us well when we're ready to let go of the Elsewhere and all we know to take the next step in our spiritual journey.

"As below, so above." If the concept applies to the relationship between our mortal plane and the spirit realm, then it also applies to relationship between the spirit world and whatever awaits above it.

What we here in this lifetime forget is that we created this reality. After all, just as we have unique traits and skills, so the needs of our personal growth are unique to each of us. It's why we're given exactly what we need. Why the teacher appears when the student is ready and not a moment before. However, if we believe that we truly created this reality, it also means that we have the power of creation at our fingertips. Magick works. We can reach the spirit world. And our limitations are only those which we choose to set in place for ourselves.

Will we achieve the fullness of that understanding in this lifetime? It's doubtful, but not impossible. It's rare that we have the opportunity to watch someone reach that portion of their path while we're walking the mortal plane. There have been stories throughout the ages of holy men and women who were capable of working what we, with our limited perspectives, perceive as miracles.

And we, if we would only let go of our boundaries and believe, are truly capable of doing even more.

The key challenge we face is in bridging the gap that exists between our accepted illusion and our spiritual birthright. We need a structure that integrates equal parts of the spirit world and physical realm into a blended whole, an approach that elevates us through summoned energy and a common language until we are capable of transitioning back and forth between the physical and spiritual unassisted.

If ritual and ceremony can be both a crutch and a boost for our faith, then it makes a great deal of sense for us to consciously utilize them as such.

When we consider the concept of ritual, especially when framed in an exploration of mystical spirituality, our thoughts generally leap to some variety of sacred ceremony. Whether it's a Catholic mass, a Wiccan Esbat, a Native American sweat lodge, or some other similar event, when we think of ritual, that's where our thoughts almost immediately travel. If we step outside of our expectations for what ritual is and can be, we may find ourselves considering weddings, birthday parties, holiday picnics and gatherings, and perhaps even court proceedings and military traditions. We rarely think of a greeting between friends, our morning coffee, or curling up with a book before drifting off to sleep.

However, ritual is all of that and much more.

In its most simplistic form, ritual is the interplay of emotion and energy in the form of communication that takes place at a point of transition. Points of transition are key as ritual could be called "the art of active manifestation." Any time we change from one chapter of our story to the next, the turning of the page involves ritual – even when we aren't consciously aware of it. Ritual can be found in the process of preparing your cup of morning coffee or tea. It's in how you say hello and good bye to friends and loved ones, in the way you prepare for work, even in how you pay for groceries at the market or prepare a meal at home.

There is a significant difference between ritual and ceremony. Ceremony is a series of actions performed in a sacred manner. Ritual is the process of energetically engaging in conscious transition from one aspect of reality to another.

At its heart, ritual is communication. This is the most misunderstood and overlooked component of ritual and is fundamental to understanding both the nature and power of this process. Each ritual we engage in speaks volumes for those who know how to hear the words it utters. Reflecting the opinions, perspective, and beliefs of the person who initiates the ritual, the ritual also communicates how that person perceives and feels about those receiving the ritual or connected to it in even the most cursory manner.

We don't need ancient incantations, secret gestures, or exotic ingredients to manifest change through ritual. As intensely powerful spiritual beings experiencing reality from a physical perspective, we already have everything that we need to manifest change at our fingertips. The secret is that we are actually engaging in the process of ritual numerous times each day.

Even with that in mind, what we lose sight of is that ritual is a gift. As the intensely powerful spiritual beings that we truly are, each ritual we engage in is a gift of ourselves. We aren't always pretty. Spirit, the very definition of love, doesn't care if we're pretty but accepts us exactly as we are. As each person, each moment that we engage in is also, due to the very definition of the concept, composed of Spirit, on some level the one receiving us also accepts us exactly as we are. Ritual is vulnerable. It's honest. It may not be a pure reflection of who we are, but it is the revealing of where we're are in that moment on our journey through Life and the evolution of our being.

The challenge comes in when we consider the role that filters play in how we see and interact with the world around us. Ritual doesn't "fail" because we weren't powerful enough. We aren't rejected in a ritual because we're not good enough. Both perceptions are based entirely on our filters.

For instance, if we are engaging in ritual and it is not having the intended results, chances are that it is our own vision that is out of sync with our higher selves. It's not as if we have a backseat driver called "our higher self" that is secretly in control. Our higher self is where our intuition. comes from. It's who we are when we remove all of our filters and we allow ourselves to fully be who we truly are. At the mercy of our filters and the way they change reality, we essentially go through life drunk on emotion – and it's our higher self, our true nature, that keeps us from making serious mistakes that will harm us in the long run.

There are two common challenges in embracing this perspective. The first is that most of us don't clearly understand what emotion is or how we react and respond to it. The second is that our typical perspective in life is much too small.

With a bit of work, we can reach a place of balance and strength where the emotional energy around us washes over us like a river coursing past a smooth stone. While we're aware of the present emotional energy, it doesn't change us or influence us. As we remove our filters, we come to clearly understand that emotional reactions are a response to energy that is not part of who we truly are. That strongly implies that the vast majority of emotion is not generated by our higher self, but is actually manifested energy around us.

As we monitor our responses and reactions to the energy in our path, we discover that not only do we stop reacting to emotion and start responding from a place of balance and strength, but that all of the emotion that we experience originates from outside of us. The only exception is love, which comes from within. Why? Because we are Divine beings and love is the very fabric of Spirit. We aren't creatures of anger; we're entities of love.

The rest of the emotion that we experience? It's manifested energy from ritual, typically interpersonal ritual where those guiding and participating in the ritual, those who were manifesting the energy and the reality accompanying it, weren't clearly aware of what they were ritually saying and were not working from a place of honesty.

We talk a lot about filters and walls on the path I teach, specifically how filters change the energy we receive based on our past experiences and how walls trap that energy within us until such time as that wall comes down and the energy is released. The trapped energy isn't pure – it's been altered by the filters we have in place. When we emotionally react to external triggers or stimuli, it is that trapped, pooled energy where our reaction comes from. Working through our walls and filters, releasing that energy a bit at a time, allows us not only to "let go" of those emotional wounds we hold onto but without the accompanying pool of energy, we find ourselves responding instead of reacting to the world around us. Our fear, insecurity, temper, worry, jealousy, anger – all of it begins to disappear. We reach a place where all that's left is love, because that's the only emotion that comes from within us.

This trapped energy, however, is very real to us. The easiest way for us to understand how strongly it affects us is to imagine it as a powerful parasite that releases hormones into our bloodstream to control us. Just as we would have to fight to maintain our center if were injected with a drug, so we struggle with the same emotional energy that we've trapped within.

The other challenge we face is one of perspective. At best we stand in a finite existence and look outward toward eternity, trying to make sense of our life and how it all fits together. To begin to understand our journey, we need to embrace the perspective of the infinite and from there, look into our finite experience in this single incarnation.

Let's say that you were in a horrible accident and lost both of your legs. Or that your spouse suddenly and unexpectedly left you. Imagine that you were just diagnosed with terminal cancer or were losing your eyesight. That you lost your home, your job, or that your best friend moved away.

All of those things are devastating, traumatic experiences when seen from our normal perspective. But imagine that you stepped outside of our normal existence and could see every moment from the instant your soul discovered awareness to the moment that it joyfully embraced once more the unity of simply being Spirit. That is a perspective that makes millennia seem like a heartbeat, that stretches beyond the understanding and scope of time itself. Now imagine that for one blink of an eye in that entire stretch of existence, in a single batting of an eyelash, that you experienced the trauma described above. The moment lasted no longer than that. From that perspective, none of that trauma would be overwhelming. It would be experienced and almost instantly forgotten in the expanse of your existence.

We see glimpses of this in our own short lifetimes. Can you remember every time you cried from the moment you were born? Each moment was traumatic enough that your tears flowed freely, but the vast majority of those moments have been lost as you've grown and evolved into the person you are today. Through a very similar process, we will outgrow the trauma we feel right now simply by continuing to reach for our higher selves.

You are not being asked to master either of these perspectives or even to fully comprehend them. What's important is that you keep them in mind as this comes through in the rituals you engage in. Where a deeply felt ritual is worked, one of two things will happen to various degrees – either you will bypass much of the stored, filtered, emotional energy that you're carrying or the ritual will tap into all of that and be heavily influenced by your past.

It is these two pieces that twist so much of the communication involved in a ritual. We have to remember that the stored, filtered energy from trauma and wounds is like a drug in our system; when we're under the influence of it we are typically incapable of seeing our actions, attitudes, and behaviors and we're influenced by this energy even years after the causative events took place. Unbalanced positive emotion, especially emotion related to personal validation, can influence our perspective, attitudes, and behavior in a very similar manner as that from a trauma or unhealed wound. To perform ritual that is an accurate mirror of our intent and our higher selves, it's imperative that we keep this concept in mind.

Why? It's very simple. We manifest reality. Each ritual is a transition, a turning of the page, and that ritual and the energy it contains has a significant role in dictating the "words" on the next chapter of our journey that we write. Start each day by saying, "I hate my life," and see how much joy you uncover. Begin each day with gratitude and appreciation and watch how your life begins to change.

This concept comes into play in all of our rituals and is essentially the most important component of effective ritual work. Before every group ritual that I lead, the very first thing we do is to go around the circle and have each member of the rite speak their intent for the ritual out loud. This process not only makes sure that all of the participants are aware of what they will be working as a group, but it causes them to stop and consider the reasons why they are there and clearly look beyond emotion and filters before they begin.

Allowing ritual to unfold without this perspective can often weave unintended energy, emotions, and outcomes into the energy we are working to manifest.

We need to stop thinking of emotion as a feeling and start thinking of it as the spiritual fabric that reality is woven from. Emotion clearly changes the way we see things.

However, it also literally changes things. In its base form, emotion is simply energy changed to carry a very specific message. And because the language of Spirit is symbolism, one of the strongest energetic languages is the language of emotion. Instead of simply being energy, it becomes laughter, jealousy, passion, hatred, fear – you can go down the list and each and every emotion is simply a manifested energetic communication. The only exception to that is love, which in my opinion, is mislabeled as an emotion. Love is Spirit, plain and simple. It's why love complete transforms what it touches. It's why love carries so much power as compared to any other emotion. It's why it comes from within us – because love, at our core, is what we are.

OOO

INTERPERSONAL RITUAL

The easiest place to see this concept in play is in interpersonal ritual. Each time we come together with another person, each of us brings our "reality bubble" with us. Where those two reality bubbles overlap, significant manifestation can occur if both parties are open to it. Remember, ritual takes place at points of transition. Even if it's subtle, every point of transition has its accompanying ritual.

For instance, visualize the following scenario:

OOO

Tom comes home from work. It's been a bear of a day and he had to work late. Tracy is already at home, having gotten off work on time.

> Tracy: You finally made it home. (She says this playfully, trying to keep the mood light as she was worried about Tom's lateness and the lack of phone call to let her know he was

working late triggered a fear that something had happened to him).

Tom (angrily): What's that supposed to mean?

Tracy (reactionary): Don't snap at me!

OOO

We've all seen this played out countless times. What we fail to realize is that this is ritual. Every time there is a transition in our world – in this case there are two, coming home from work and being reunited with a loved one – we engage in ritual. In that moment we are energetically placing the words that will be read on the next page of our story.

On an energetic level, the following is how each person interacted with the energy, based on their limited perspective and the filters and stored energy they carried with them. Remember, emotion is energy and ritual simply communication. The words have been changed, not to hold their true meaning, but to illustrate how each person received them.

OOO

Tracy: It's about time you made it home. You're late. You were nagged all day at work and home isn't any different. You're going to be nagged here too.

Tom (angrily): I am not the slightest bit happy to see you because my insecurity tells me you're finding fault in me, just like my nit-picking boss.

Tracy (reactionary): Don't reject me!

OOO

Our emotions and our filters are literally that powerful. One of the things that we have to keep in mind is that the person who initiates a ritual has, by default, become the guide for that ritual. In this particular situation, it would take massive amounts of conscious energy for Tom to change the course of ritual, not because he lacks responsibility for it, but because Tracy, as the initiator of the exchange, has unknowingly taken the role of guide. Tom would not only have to reverse the flow of the ritual and take the role of guide, but Tracy, as the initiator, would have to allow him to do so, whether that decision was conscious or a subconscious process.

This is one of the challenges that many parents face with their children. When an interaction takes place, the child has typically already initiated the ritual – and by doing so, has unknowingly placed themselves in the role of the guide for that ritual. As parents, we need to consciously exert the energy to assume the role of guide in mid-flow, rather than simply responding to the energy the child is creating or allowing them to continue to dictate how the ritual will flow.

It's also one of the reasons why abuse, in any form, becomes so damaging. If personal interaction is simply ritual, then the abuser either initiates the ritual or continues to press the issue until they take over as guide. When we remember that ritual is communication and creates a transition, the messages that this sort of interaction sends are very damaging to both parties involved, but particularly to the non-abuser.

Going back to Tom and Tracy and using the concepts we've considered this far, it's up to Tracy as the guide of the ritual to step back, gain perspective, and consider the filters in play in herself (she's not responsible for Tom's filters) and how they will influence the scenario before she engages in ritual. The thing most people miss about filters is that the energy flows through them in both directions, the filter changing the energy from what is offered to what we perceive when it's received and changing it in the same manner from what we intend to what we project. In this case, Tom and Tracy have a strong, loving relationship and Tracy realizes that she can project that strength and love as well as receiving it. Realizing that she was worried about Tom (fear, being an emotion, is a filter) because he didn't call, she considers the filter it creates and works around it.

OOO

Tracy: I'm glad you're home safe. (She gives Tom a hug and looks up lovingly and worried at him). You didn't call and when you were late, I was scared something happened to you.

Tom: I'm sorry I didn't call. It was a rough day, but I'm glad I'm finally home.

Tracy: I'm glad you are too.

OOO

Honesty is critically important in all ritual work. If you can't find the center of honesty to work from, don't do the ritual. It's that simple. Tracy didn't have to pretend she was okay. She didn't have to pretend that she wasn't scared. In the first example, by saying, "You finally made it home," even though she was trying to make the exchange seem playful, it was actually somewhat accusatory. This is why Tom reacted the way that he did. In the final example, he's still grumpy from his day, but the interaction is pure.

The other thing to keep in mind is that there are two rituals involved here – coming home from work and being reunited with a spouse. As Tom was nearing home, he was also nearing a transition point in his world. Just as Tracy needed to step back and consider the energy in play before that transition point, Tom needs to do the same thing before he steps through the door and engages in ritual. Had he done so, his reaction would have been reduced to a response and he would have been in position to assume the role of guide had it been necessary and Tracy was willing to relinquish that role.

Trust clearly becomes an extremely important factor when engaging in ritual. If you have significant trust issues – in yourself, the other person, in Spirit – those issues are going to manifest in the rituals you engage in.

One of the key components to consider is that the one who initiates the ritual, the guide, is not only starting the ritual, but they are establishing the energy that both parties have to at their disposal to craft the ritual.

SACRED RITUAL

While these concepts may seem obvious in interpersonal ritual, it's exactly the same scenario in sacred ritual when working magick, praying, or interacting with the spirit world. When you start a ritual, even what we tend to refer to as a solitary ritual, you are not doing it alone. Whether you are working with Spirit, the spirit world, or the symbolism of your own subconscious, when you initiate ritual, you become the guide for the rite. The energy that you establish is the energy that both sides of that equation will work with.

Honesty isn't only key, it's imperative. Dishonest ritual will not work. There may be some result, but it will not be what you intended, simply because the starting energy wasn't honest. To think of it in very simplistic terms, honesty means "the truth is the same"; dishonesty means "the truth is different." When we work an honest ritual, when we are balanced with our higher self, when our perspective sees the greater picture, when we guide the process in honesty, we are telling reality, "I want the outcome to be the same as this rite." When we don't do these things, we're telling reality, "I want the outcome to be different than this rite." We are the guide and the energy we use defines the rite. As we've already discovered on this journey together, symbolism is truly the language of magick.

What's more is that in our example of Tom and Tracy, if we substitute Tom (simply because he's did not initiate the ritual) with Spirit, when our energy is unbalanced and coming from a place of mistrust and dishonesty, Spirit will attempt to take the role of guide in our ritual work and what we're manifesting. We do not have to allow that to happen – and most of us can attest to having fought that exact process – but the attempt will take place.

STRUCTURED RITUAL

To work ritual in a structured manner requires an understanding of the energetic process involved in that ritual. A structured ritual, at its heart, is what is commonly known as "sympathetic magick." An easier way of understanding this concept would be to call it "mirrored reality." In a structured ritual, we seek to create an energetic process that mirrors what we wish to see as the manifested outcome.

For instance, let's say you were creating a ritual to have more money come into your life. As part of the ritual, you could draw or write an amount on a piece of paper and place it inside an envelope with an actual dollar or two. (Two dollars would be perfect as the number three - the written amount and the two single dollar bills - is a manifestation number. The easiest way to remember this concept is the phrase, "One is an anomaly. Two is a coincidence. Three is a pattern." Establishing a symbolic pattern creates a stronger energetic concept than not doing so). In the rite, you would open up the envelope, "receive" the money, and give thanks for it. If you're looking for a specific amount, saying, "Thank you for," and stating the amount, "of money," will establish that energetic bond. You can do the same with a pay raise at work.

While there is some debate over the ethics of working ritual for gain, a need is a need. If you're following the lead of your higher self, clearly seeing the bigger picture, and working without filters, the ritual will be effective. If you're missing any of these points, it won't work.

CHAPTER EIGHT

THE ELEMENTS OF RITUAL

I stand before the mirror, looking at my half-asleep eyes and my unshaven face. It's early morning and the workday beckons insistently. My body is filled with sunlight, pulled from another beautiful sunrise, and my spirit is at ease from welcoming and thanking a new day. But there is yet another ritual to be done, one I do every weekday morning.

It's time to shave.

I slip my hands into the warm water that partially fills the sink, closing my eyes as I center myself. As I raise my cupped hands to my face, as I bask in the wet heat of the first touch of water on my unshaven skin, I picture the Element of Air, entering my body with the warmth of the water. Today I choose the memory of a ritual I did on a lonely windswept beach outside of San Francisco, reliving the beauty of the night, the moonlight coloring the waves with pale hues. As I feel the touch of water, as I summon the Element of Air with my cupped hands, I remember the ocean wind, the way it whipped through my hair, the way it danced around me. And as I call upon it once more, I feel Air filling me, refreshing me, preparing me for a new day.

With each caress of water, I call upon another element, reconnecting it to my being. Fire is the light of my match, the single candle that I nestled in the protected arms of a pocket of stone, sheltering the fragile flame. Water is the sea, the waves surging past the outcrop of stone I stand on, its power echoing in the roar of the surf. Earth is the stone beneath my feet, the rocks that extend out into the power of the Pacific Ocean. Spirit is the voices on the wind, the presence of the sea, the spark of life I carry within.

I'm no longer simply preparing to shave; I'm a practitioner with the power of the natural world at my fingertips.

It may seem silly at first, to instill something as mundane as shaving with a bit of magick, but the results are as potent as the most elaborate ceremony. Once again, each transition is a ritual. Our days are filled with rituals, little things we do the same way each day without thinking, ruled by habit and the prodding of our subconscious minds.

Think about the dish you set your car keys in when you come home from work. Is it simply so you can find them in the morning? Or is it a subconscious symbol that you're home, that you're stepping from the workday world into the embrace of the hearth? Or take, for instance, your morning coffee. Do you drink it simply for the taste or is it a tool you use to mentally prepare you for your day, the rush of caffeine the jump start you need to face the morning commute and the first hours in the office?

Our days are filled with countless transitions, with minute ceremonies that are more than simple routine. We simply don't stop to think about why we do these things. Why did I instinctively use five handfuls of water to wet my face to shave? Was my face wetter than with just one? Did it make the razor sharper or the shaving cream more lubricating? As I stopped and thought about it, I realized that subconsciously I was pausing before the sink each morning to prepare myself to enter the flow of the work day, that in those few moments I was transitioning from the home to work, that it was a final deep breath before leaping into my day. By stopping and trying to understand the rituals in my life, I was able to move their significance from my subconscious to conscious mind. And by purposely honoring and embracing the rituals that my subconscious created, I was able to instill my immediate awareness with those things that I instinctively knew I needed.

When we begin to look at ritual, regardless of whether it is a magickal ceremony or a mundane moment in life, we slowly begin to realize that most rituals are composed of eight simple stages. Sometimes we may combine steps together; occasionally we may exclude one or two altogether. But more often than not, all eight of the steps outlined below are present in both our daily rituals and our magickal rites.

STEP ONE: CLEANSING

The first step in ritual, cleansing, is more than simply a matter of purifying ourselves or a ritual area. It's a subconscious process of setting aside one type of energy or state of mind and transitioning to a new one. When I'm preparing to work an indoor magickal ceremony, I will often symbolically cleanse the room that I'll be using. I begin by physically cleaning the room, tidying it with the same care I would as if I were going to entertain a guest. Next, I take a broom and symbolically sweep the old energy away, creating a blank energetic template with which to work the rite. This is followed by a focused visualization as I slowly smudge every surface of the room with smoldering white sage, cleansing and purifying the room. This process isn't simply a matter of cleaning a room or removing old energy. What I'm doing is creating a transition from one state of being to another.

It's important to keep in mind that there isn't "negative" energy that needs to be removed so that we can work ritual; the entire intent is to allow us to let go of one energetic state to embrace another. The ritual itself won't improve exponentially by moving from not sweeping the carpet to ritual sweeping, from ritual sweeping to physical vacuuming, and from vacuuming to deep cleaning with a carpet shampooer. Until we've reached the point that we can remove ritual as a crutch in our workings, we need to be aware of what each step does to our own inner energetic state. We will naturally progress from sweeping and smudging to achieving the same energetic space through a single deep breath and then by simply willing it to be. However, much like training a musician first to read music, then to play a few simple notes, before working up to more complex rhythms and phrasing, so we also need to train ourselves to work magick.

Think of energetic process behind cleansing this way. Imagine that you are in a room with a single, soiled window. The light barely filters through the grime; the room is dim and dark, four walls and an opaque window that define our reality. As we take a cloth to the window, we aren't simply removing the dirt. Sunlight begins to filter through the glass, changing the lighting of the room, the brightness subconsciously changing our perspective and our mood. As we continue to wipe the dirt from the glass, what were simply dark shadows before becomes a tree branch filled with the new leaves of late spring.

If we were to only look at the process from a mundane perspective, we simply see what is immediately before us - we removed the grime and made the window clean. But to work magick means to think of all of reality as being composed of Spirit, to think of each interaction as ritual, and to think of the transitions, connections, communication, as they blend into the larger weave around us, rather than focusing on the isolated individual parts. Instead of the window being a separate entity, it becomes a part of a larger whole. The process of cleaning the window is no longer simply a process of removing dirt. It is a process of transformation, changing our immediate reality, the room we stand in, from something dismal and secluded into a world filled with light and the whispers of spring.

The first step in ritual isn't simply a matter of cleansing away the old - it's a process of transition, moving from one state of energy to another.

STEP TWO: SETUP

This is the process of preparing ourselves or our physical space to carry out the rite. In step one, we "cleansed" the energy so we could begin something new, so we could step from one type of energy to another. "Setup" is the process of gathering the tools (real or symbolic) that we need to continue with the rite; it's the bringing of the elements we need together so that we are prepared to take the step forward that initiates the process. This differs from "raising energy" (explained below) which is much more active. It's easiest to think of this second step as continuing to change the room where we cleaned the window above. Imagine that it's a small room in a house you're renovating, that you want to set this room aside exclusively for magickal work and indoor ritual. Cleansing would involve washing the windows, sweeping the floors, and removing the last traces of what the room had been used for before and beginning the shift into something new. In the setup portion of the ritual, you would gather the paints and brushes, spread your drop cloth, and bring in a stereo with a tape of your favorite music.

Although it may not seem so at first glance, this often precedes "intent" (below). We have yet to take that step from planning to doing. Our materials may be gathered, but subconsciously we still haven't focused on the creative process, the actual implementing of our plan. For many of the daily rituals we naturally go through, "cleansing" and "setup" are subconscious processes. You can think of cleansing as the moment that exists between ending of one period where you are consciously or subconsciously embracing a specific type of energy and the beginning of another, and setup as the planting of a seed to begin the new process. I've found in my life that, as I'm beginning to work toward a new goal, that I often find myself subconsciously studying related materials for weeks or even months before I actually begin.

STEP 3: INTENT

Once we have prepped the moment in "cleansing" and "setup," we are ready to make a final decision on what we're going to do with the energy. Intent is the moment most of us recognize as the beginning, the moment that the seed we planted begins to grow, to reach toward the sun and we begin to reach toward our goal. In the example of our room, it's the decision that dips the brush into the paint, that says with a smile, "Let's do this." It's the moment when the energy changes from one state to another.

If you're new to magick, you may be asking yourself, "What's all this talk about energy? Isn't energy something that you simply use in spellwork?" It's true that energy is a fundamental component of spellwork, but it is more than just that. We've already considered how everything is composed of Spirit (or, more accurately, how everything is Spirit). From this point forward, as you begin to engage in magick and ritual, you will begin to realize how interconnected all of life is, that the energy we raise for our magickal rites is always present, that it is at the very core of our existence. Think of how you feel when you're upset and how you feel when you're not. Or how the sensation of your being feels when you're intently focused on a task or when you're relaxing and spending time with close friends. As you begin to pay attention to your life, you'll realize that your entire being goes through various states of energy throughout your day. The mental shift and accompanying change of energy that occurs when I prepare to go to work in the morning simply isn't there on a day off. There isn't that transition, that change from one state of being to another. And consequently, there is no morning ritual that takes me from a lazy Saturday morning to a carefree Saturday afternoon, simply because I don't require one. Why? Because I'm not creating a dramatic shift in energy.

And that's what a great deal of our ritual is about. When we cast a circle, we're seeking to move beyond the energy of the mundane world, to move between the worlds, to dramatically change the energy around us. For those of us who have participated in athletics, we know that there's a shift in consciousness in that period of time where we're preparing ourselves to compete. Every athlete has rituals they use to prepare for a competition: a specific visualization, a pattern of breathing, a certain way to untie and tie their track shoes. None of these things would be valuable if they didn't usher in a change of energy, a specific transition from one state of being to another.

Intent is the deep breath we take as we approach the starting blocks, the dipping of the brush in the paint, that moment when we sit down and find the inspiration to reach for the first word to type in a manuscript.

STEP 4: RAISING ENERGY

For anyone who has cast a typical modern circle, this is the stage where you call the Quarters, raise energy for the rite and begin to weave the ritual from the components you've chosen to use. As we begin to raise energy, we take that conscious step from making the decision to pursue a certain path to actually implementing the change. In the example of the room we're renovating, we begin to actually apply the paint to the walls, using combinations of colors to slowly change the reality of the room. If it were a magickal ceremony we were performing, this would be where we summoned the energy to our task.

To picture this process, imagine that you're teaching a lesson to a group of people. To cleanse, you've taken the visualizations that you've done over the past few days, the mental preparation, and summoned it to the forefront of your mind, bringing forth that state of consciousness that you will need to effectively teach those in attendance. You've gathered the visual aids you will need and a glass of water to keep your voice fresh as a matter of setting up. As you focus your intent, you think of exactly what you are intending to do. Is it simply a matter of speaking in front of a group of people without being nervous or do you seek to impart a bit of knowledge to them that they can use in their daily lives? As you step before them, you begin to interact with the energy of the group. Each sentence receives a reaction, no matter how subtle, that a skilled speaker can read. Do you need to ask them questions that will draw them into the lesson, that will weave their answers into the process and make them a part of the class? Have you begun to establish a rapport with them that will enable your intent to take life?

Raising energy is the step from simply intending to make a change to actually interacting with the energy that is involved in that change. It is the process of moving from merely wanting or intending to reach toward a specific goal, and actually taking the steps to reach it.

STEP 5: APPLYING ENERGY

In the example of our room renovation, when we raised energy, we began to paint the room, adding new colors to the world around us. But at this point they are merely brighter hues on a dim canvas, they are simply colors without form, without substance, and without a precisely defined role.

It's at this point where we begin to apply the energy, to take the colors that we've brought to the room and slowly weave them into something beautiful. We carefully tape the window's glass and, with a smaller brush, bring new life to a faded window frame. We might paint the floorboards a complimentary color or decide to put a new plate on the light switch. But even though it may seem that we are simply continuing the process outlined in raising energy, we are now doing something more.

First of all, we're present and very aware, living completely in the moment. That is key to magick and one of the secrets behind the first four steps. We didn't shift the ritual space around us into some magickal otherland; we shifted our own energy and awareness into ritual space.

But as we begin to apply the energy, we find ourselves doing something that is truly beautiful and very magickal.

We're creating.

If you talk to an artist, they'll tell you that their finished work often turns out quite differently than they originally intended. That, as they begin to work, they may become inspired by new colors or decide that the piece seems to be leading them in a new direction. There is a fragile, undefined moment when a process stops becoming a mental exercise and begins to take on a life of its own. In the example of our room, we may find ourselves smiling as we can suddenly see how the room is taking shape. It is no longer something we simply intended to do, it is no longer a process of moving from one state of energy to another. We are there, we are embracing the energy we've created, and in the next step, we will seal it and make it strong.

This stage, applying energy, is that moment when "it all comes together." If you've done a certain amount of magickal ritual work, you know that in your ceremonies there comes a time when everything begins to flow, when it seems as if there is an unseen wind at your back, filling your magickal sails. There simply comes that moment when it all begins to fall into place and, subconsciously, we begin to approach the process with a new state of mind. No longer are we simply trying to create something - we are actually creating, we can see the process coming to life before our eyes.

But, if you pay attention to what's going on inside you, we don't stop what we're doing at this point. We are within the flow of energy, we have stepped from one state of being to another. We are no longer simply a person with mundane concerns, with a thousand questions about who we are and why we're here. We're the artist, creating something that gives us joy; the athlete, seeing all of our training pay off; the musician, at one with the music, feeling it flow. Or the home owner, smiling in pride as an old dismal room begins to come to life and slowly forms into something magickal beneath our touch. We are completely present and fully in the moment. That is one of the key secrets behind working successful magick.

STEP 6: SEALING ENERGY

Our room is painted and beautiful, the windows open, letting in the cool breeze of spring. But if you think back, that wasn't our intent. We wanted to reclaim the room, to make it a special place devoted to ritual and ceremony within our home. In the current moment, the freshly painted room is simply that - a bright, cheerful room. If we were to walk away, to leave it in its current state, its purpose may change. It may sit, unused, until we begin using it for storage, to keep the empty boxes that once contained the household we've unpacked into our new home. The room itself is ready, we simply have to take the final step, to seal it into its intended purpose.

Sealing the energy is the "lock" of the ritual, a process of binding the energy to a spell or taking the steps to insure an endeavor is successful. It's the handshake on a deal; the "As I speak, so shall it be" in spellwork.

This sealing is important for two reasons. First of all, it creates a subconscious shift within us. In the example of the room, we have only created something beautiful that we intended to be used for a specific purpose. But we have yet to name the creation, to give it life, to welcome it into its new role. By naming the room or presenting it with its purpose, we define it. The work of art is no longer a simple painting but, "A Morning With Roses." The room is no longer simply a beautiful room beginning with the moment when we stop and say, "I have created this room for ritual and ceremony. And it is complete."

So what is involved in sealing energy?

It can actually be a very simple process. When most people do spellwork, they stop the process after directing the energy to its destination. Sealing the energy is simply visualizing it actually accomplishing it's task and saying something like, "As I speak, so shall it be," claiming the completion of the spell and sealing that completion to the energy you just directed.

Think of it like this. Let's say you're at the beach and you want to fill a bottle with seawater. Rather than just dunking it in the ocean until it's filled, you dig a little indentation in the sand and lay the bottle on its side with the mouth facing the surf. As the waves come crashing in, some of the seawater gets into the bottle while some of it erodes the sand, so the mouth of the bottle points down at a slight angle. If the seawater was the energy of the rite and the bottle was where you were directing it, you'll notice that while the water goes into the bottle with each wave, a portion of it also pours out because the bottle is tilted downward. Sealing the energy (by visualizing the spell to its completion) is kind of like waiting for a wave to fill the bottle and then sticking a cork in it before the water can run out. I like to say something similar to, "As I speak, so shall it be," as a way of saying, "I got the cork in! And water, you're going to stay in there!" The verbal component is not completely necessary, but there is a certain power to the spoken word and every little bit helps.

I always have a purpose behind every ritual I do - magickal or otherwise. This is the intent we speak. Even if I am simply casting a circle to honor the moon, I will specifically focus on honoring the moon within that circle. In a situation such as that, I may spend some time focusing on the moon, visualizing its energy filling me and then to seal it, I might visualize that as I turn my face away from the moon, I remain filled with the moon's glowing light, that I can still feel its presence even though my eyes are no longer on it. I might say something simple like, "Even when I can't see you, Moon, I am still connected to you and filled with your light."

Sealing the energy is the period at the end of the sentence, the moment when we realize that our task is complete, that we claim the victorious outcome as our own. But we aren't done yet. There are still two very important steps to complete.

STEP 7: GIVING THANKS

I was taught, both by teachers and by monitoring my own state of mind while working doing ritual work, that we should always give thanks. This is as fundamental to me as grounding energy at the end of a rite and is a lesson that I seek to instill in every student that I work with.

There are a number of reasons why we give thanks, but I believe the most important is that it begins to change our perspective and our attitude toward all of life. When we thank someone, even ourselves, it implies that what was done has value, that it's important. Try thanking yourself for a job well done. It's amazing how it changes the way you think and feel. When you thank the natural world for a wonderful day of hiking, you will stop seeing the forest as merely dirt and trees, but rather a special, interwoven creation which provided you with the memories of the day, with the energy of the afternoon, and with the spiritual recharging that so many of us find outdoors.

Giving thanks implies that we received something, rather than simply taking it. As we move deeper into our paths and begin working with spirits, both natural and ethereal, you'll realize how much of your ability to interconnect with them has to do with your frame of mind. It is a little understood, seldom mentioned area of magick, but one which impacts your ability to consciously manifest change as much as anything else.

The process of giving thanks can be simple or elaborate. It can take the shape of a quiet moment or a gift we give the energy around us. Think back to the magickal room we've been renovating in these pages. It has changed from a dismal corner of our house to an enchanted place to create ritual and magick. To say thanks, we could simply stand in the doorway, admiring the colors of the fresh painted room, basking in the caress of the wind and the sunlight that spills through the open window and say, "Thank you room, for coming to life." We could then turn and thank ourselves for bringing something beautiful to our home. We could allow our thanks to take a physical form, bringing a bouquet of flowers from our garden in to further enliven the energy around us.

As we begin to be thankful for the various rituals within our lives, we begin to understand the value of each sacred moment. The path I teach focuses on awakening to life; it seeks to teach us to open our eyes to the life we live. If you could give yourself one gift, would it be a car? A house? Or the ability to look back upon each day, seeing it as richly lived, feeling that we truly experienced what it means to be alive? Giving thanks is a fundamental part of this process, which is a gift to ourselves precious beyond compare.

STEP 8: GROUNDING

When we work ritual, we specifically take hold of the energy of a moment and move it from one state of being to another. We have gone from early morning at home to the chaotic rush of the morning commute. We've taken a dingy room and turned it into something beautiful. Or perhaps we've cast a circle and woven the energy into a spell. Whatever the purpose, we've connected ourselves to the energy of the moment. By taking charge of the situation, we've bound our being to the things we've changed.

Remember, we work ourselves into every single one of our rituals.

The energy involved in any ritual has a definite, often subtle impact on our daily lives. Occasionally, we will specifically choose not to ground. There are a number of reasons that we may seek to do this; for instance a rite which connects our sick body to healing energy. But normally we seek to let go of one type of energy, so we can begin to embrace another. This process is as important in a magickal ceremony as it is finding closure when ending a job or a relationship.

Grounding is simple and there are countless ways to do it. After a magickal rite, I often stomp my feet or eat a bit of food. Both shift the subconscious back to the realm of the physical. If neither method is appropriate, I will often say something simple, such as, "I let go of the moment, freeing myself from all but the wisdom and memories it contains."

Breaking a ritual into eight stages may not seem important. But this is a useful concept for us to use for two reasons.

First of all, it helps us break the event down into understandable portions. We can't begin to fully embrace something until we can understand it. That's one of the probable reasons why our spiritual ancestors sought out the solstices and equinoxes; they divided the solar year into portions that they could understand. It is much simpler to grasp the change of energy from the summer solstice to autumnal equinox, than it is when we have no point of reference. When the seasons are undefined, when do you plant? With a nebulous solar year, how do you know when the fish will begin running or the game return?

Our lives are a lot like that. How can we understand our own flow unless we begin to gain perspective regarding the flow of our energy? If you find yourself growing tired at a certain time of day, your mood regularly changing for reasons you don't understand, or another shift in consciousness taking place at regular intervals, stop and take a look at your world. Consider what is happening before, during, and after each step. It's likely you will find transitions there that can be embraced ritualistically. By doing so, you can begin to understand why you respond in certain ways. And anything that you understand, you can fully embrace or change as you see fit.

The second reason is that, by understanding the components of ritual, we can create new rituals as we require them.

CHAPTER NINE

CIRCLE WORK

Almost from our very first moments on a magickal path, many of us are taught that our magick and rituals need to be performed within a Circle - a defined area where we interact with magickal energies. We cast a Circle through various means. Some of us use an athame, a magickal knife, to describe the boundaries of our sacred space. Others invite the Quarters, elemental energies from the four directions. This concept is not only valid, but incredibly useful.

Unfortunately, it's also flawed - not in theory, but in scope.

We truly need to understand that we are spiritual beings living a physical experience. If you think back on the material from an earlier point in this book, you may realize that if each of us is Divine, then by extension we innately have the power of creation at our fingertips. The only thing that holds us back are the limitations that we set in place when we came into this lifetime, limitations that we can consciously let go of in order to embrace the fullness of our power and our birthright as spiritual beings.

Following the path that I was taught, both by physically incarnated teachers and those who are currently teaching from the Elsewhere, what we consider "circle casting" is one example of how a concept can be applied. The unfortunate truth is that very few of us are taught anything beyond that point, including the theory and application of the concepts behind circle work. It's as if someone along the way found an old grimoire whose pages had been damaged by water, burned by fire, torn by earth, and scattered by air. Pages were missing leading up to the rite of circle casting and the book was too damaged to read beyond that point. So the reader, attempting the approach outlined in the grimoire, found it to be useful and taught it to others.

"It is apparent that you work magick in a circle," they said. "You've got to try it! It works."

And it does work.

However, the concept is similar to someone offering to teach you how to make breakfast and walking you through the process of making cold cereal. You take an empty bowl and a spoon, fill the bowl with cereal and add milk. Voila! Breakfast is made.

So you teach the next person, not calling it "cold cereal" but calling it "breakfast." Then someone decides to try adding fruit to sweeten it and a handful of berries are tossed into the mix. The debate becomes "berries versus no berries" until someone decides they like their cereal dry and eats it without milk. We begin to eat it out of special bowls and use sacred spoons that have been handed down throughout the ages.

But there's more to breakfast than cold cereal, just as there is more to ritual magick than a cast circle.

THE BASICS

In its simplest form, a circle is both a laboratory and a painter's canvas. You're undertaking a twofold process - a duality that is both precise and divided while also being creative and inclusive. First, you're creating energetically neutral space and separating it from the world around you so that the only energy that enters this space is that which you consciously intend to be part of the rite. Second, you're taking the building blocks of reality and spinning them into thread, much like wool is spun into yarn. Everything beyond this point is purely dependent on the intent of the ritual that's being undertaken.

Casting a circle is a surefire approach to this process. That's why it works. You ritually cleanse the area and then lock it off from the rest of reality. In this energetically neutral space, you pull in the concepts that you want to weave and set to work. The woven energy is then placed back into the flow of reality (the applied intent of your ritual) and then you open up the space and ground yourself back in the mundane flow of things.

The grounding portion of this process is tremendously important because a part of you is attached to the energy you wove and placed back into the flow of reality. Casting a circle literally put you in neutral territory - you're not in the spirit world, you're "between the worlds," nestled in one of the seams of reality. Remember, you are a part of every ritual you work. A simple way of understanding the connection is to imagine that, as the weaver of the rite, you're covered in the energy you wove, much like a baker's hands are covered in flour. The only difference is that instead of leaving powdery white hand prints if you don't "ground" by washing up after cooking, in circle casting you become one of the ingredients. As your magick draws energy to it, it also draws your energy into the mix. Because this is happening between the worlds and your energy is still connected to the rite, in a very real sense you're still between the worlds as well. That's why we often feel dizzy or light-headed after working a rite when we fail to ground. We're still connected to it.

While our typical approach to casting a circle is an effective way to work magick, it's only one way of doing so - and our techniques and abilities may not be as effective as we'd like.

STEPPING BETWEEN THE WORLDS

Magickal practitioners are the hackers of physical reality. We see beyond the software of mundane reality and change its code. But anyone who has ever done any programming knows, you can't do it without accessing the program's code so you can alter and recompile it.

There's a place between the "user" and the "machine," an area where the code of reality is written. That's where we do our work, in the seams of reality. I used to work with a group of pagans who would declare as part of their circle casting, "We're between the worlds, beyond the realm of time, where life and death, fear and love, light and darkness exist as one." It's this place, this in-between, that we seek to reach when we work circle-based magick.

Casting a Circle is extremely useful for one reason and one reason only - it allows us to physically accompany our spirit in the process of weaving magickal energy. Magick relies heavily symbolism. That's why we can use a stone to represent the entire Elemental concept of Earth or a feather to represent all of the manifestations and potential of Air. If we were working a purely spirit-based rite, we could use shamanic journeying techniques to enter into our inner sanctuary and work the rite there, not moving a muscle, not needing a single physical component. But we step between the worlds when we do Circle-based magick. We're right in the center of reality's seam, in a space between physical reality and the spirit realm. It's our intent that what we're weaving will manifest both in the subtle flow of reality and in our mundane lives. For this process to work at all, we have to symbolically incorporate both our spirit and our physical self in the rite.

REMOVING THE CRUTCH

When I teach a student in the offline world, I use what I jokingly refer to as the spiral method. We take a concept, learn it and move on to the next concept, each building on the one before. I require the student to stretch their boundaries, to let go of old tools and develop abilities and a level of proficiency by stepping away from the structure of a concept and working with only their own energy. Just about the time we get to the point where they're really comfortable in letting go, we go back to the concepts we let go of long ago and the student is encouraged to use them with their new level of ability. In this way we spiral along the path, coming back to a concept only to leave it behind once more, spiraling ever upward.

There's an old story of a young man who was accepted to study martial arts at a renown monastery. He proudly left his village behind to study under the guidance of a great kung fu master. Much to his dismay, the master gave him a single task - to stand before a rain barrel and strike the surface of the water with his open palm until he'd splashed all the water from the barrel. When the barrel was empty, it was refilled and the student began anew, day after day after day.

During a major holiday, the student was allowed to return to his village, where the townsfolk were eager to hear all that he'd learned and see a demonstration of his newly honed abilities.

"I've learned nothing!" He exclaimed, angrily slapping the thick wooden table with his open hand.

The table split in half under his single blow.

And the student understood what the master was trying to teach him.

The core concepts of magick are incredibly simple - it's the application of those concepts that are as varied, complex, and unique as the people who work the rites. When we work with a concept, like circle casting, it's important that we don't rely on it as the only way to do something or we will never grow beyond that level. Just like a child, first we learn to crawl, then we learn to walk, then we learn to run. And just like a child learns to let go of the security of using their hands to crawl and trusts their legs to hold them upright, so we too need to step beyond our comfort zone, begin reducing the components of our rituals, and move the energy without them.

If we can do this, we find ourselves with the same astonishment as the martial arts student. Honing our abilities, we find that when we need to use a fully cast circle for a rite, that the rite is incredibly powerful. Instead of the elements of our ritual allowing us to reach a certain level of reality, we find that they empower us to move beyond that level.

A NATURAL PROGRESSION

There is a natural progression to everything within magick. What's more is that each concept in magick holds a secret. As we begin to explore the concept fully, we discover hidden insight and power within that concept. Stepping into our new understanding, we discover that there's another secret that awaits beyond our newly won place on the path. And a secret beyond that. And beyond that.

Most of us begin our journey by working with a fully cast circle, following instructions laid out in a book, offered by a teacher, or created on our own. But this is just the first step in the journey of learning how to hone magickal ability. Remember, the key reason why we use a circle for magick is that it symbolically allows our physical body to enter the rite, mirroring our intent to have our magick manifest on both the perceived spiritual and mundane levels of reality.

When I teach students how to cast a circle, we pull out all the stops. Candles are placed at the four Quarters and are lit when Fire is called into the Circle. Water is sprinkled around the boundary we describe, as is salt to represent Earth. We use either a small set of chimes, a tiny bell, or an ancient Tibetan singing bowl for Air. Energy is pulled in and directed. We invoke and evoke. Tools and symbolic elements are utilized. It's a complex and very ritualistic process.

The next step is to let go of the tools while utilizing the same concepts. I'll often have the student pull energy in from the air around them and shape it into thick cords. When the student is capable of creating three energy cords simultaneously and weaving them into a single rope, we then direct the energy rope in a circle around us, defining the ritual area in this manner. This teaches the student to energetically create and maintain sacred space.

The next time we need to use a circle, we will use four candles set at the Quarters and nothing more. The student is expected to be able to successfully cast a circle using only these tools and a flame, utilizing their newly honed ability to create and maintain energetic space.

Taking an additional step away from ritual, we move to using only a single candle flame, the student connecting to the circle of candlelight and energetically following it and enhancing it to create their ritual space.

Then, in the most difficult of this series of exercises, we sit motionlessly, eyes open, in full light, and without moving create energetic space, letting go of the need to pull the energy in, shape it into cords and weave it into a rope. Without motion, without words, without physical components, we simply will the ritual to take place.

When a student has shown aptitude in all of these stages, we return to a fully cast circle. With mastery over each of the elements involved in the process of creating circular ritual space, the rite itself is greatly enhanced and they're capable of moving, sustaining, and directing significantly greater amounts of energy within the rite.

And once circle casting has been mastered once more, we move to working with instant circles - shifting from mundane to magickal space and immediately manifesting energy without the need for a rite.

WHY A CIRCLE?

It's symbolically necessary to use a circle when working magick. That's not to say that we need to cast a circle each time, but that we need to be in a defined energetically neutral space and that we need to be near the center of that space when we're spinning the energy into threads and weaving it into reality. The circle doesn't have to be formal and it need be no bigger than is required to enclose our physical body. But because of the symbolism of us working a change that will appear both in the perceived spiritual and physical realms, we need to have both our body (physical) and energy (spirit) present to empower the rite.

A circle is a paradox, much like the fabric of reality. In magick, there is no such thing as linear time, although we, as human beings, clearly perceive a "before", a "during", and an "after" to each of the events of our lives. When we cast a circle, there's a moment when we begin and when we are finished, but once in place, a circle simply exists. It has no beginning and no end. There is no "head" of the circle.

There is no starting point or end point. The circle simply is. Because magick is a tremendously symbolic undertaking, the more completely the symbolism of our weaving reflects the fullness of what we're doing in the ritual, the more effective our rite will be.

Second, energy flows like water. Imagine that you were able to physically direct the flow of water. What would happen if you were trying to contain it in a large square and that energy encountered a corner? In a circular energetic environment, there is nothing to interrupt the flow of energy and cause it to "ripple" or create symbolic dissonance.

The third and final reason is a combination of the first two. Reality is formed of spheres. We can see this reflected throughout mundane reality. When we look up at the night sky, we see the celestial sphere, a perceived sphere on which the stars, planets, the moon, and such are reflected. When we speak of a governments and world affairs, we talk about their sphere of influence. We might refer to a person's network of relationships as their social sphere.

If we were to step completely outside of our mundane senses, we'd discover that this is also true on a magickal or spiritual level. Each of us creates our own sphere of reality. If you're in energetic balance, you can reach out and sense the world around you equidistant in every direction. That's your sphere. If you were to stretch your arms out like the wings of a bird, your reality sphere extends to just about the tips of your fingers. Reality isn't an even plane, but a series of overlapping spheres that create a seamless whole. Because there are so many individual overlapping spheres, and we're capable of perceiving the energy of those we interact with, we see this conglomeration of individual spherical realities as a composite, rather than as its individual pieces.

HOW IT WORKS

When we cast a circle, in whatever form we choose, we're essentially creating a new sphere. We're inside that sphere, constructing it out of the energy we pull in and from our own personal energy. That's why we define the boundaries of our circle. That's why we need energetically neutral space. When we cast our spell, work our magick, or perform our rite, we're symbolically pushing the sphere we've created into the midst of the greater network of spheres with the intent to influence reality, much as our own definition of reality influences the world around us.

Doing so, we're not only between the worlds, bringing a new sphere to life, but we're stepping into a middle ground, half in our own personal sphere, half in the Elsewhere. That's why it's so important that we ground when we finish a rite. Because just as we influence the flow of reality, so it can influence us once we release the boundaries of our circle. We will naturally integrate back into our own sphere over time, but dizziness, light-headedness, lack of focus, and (occasionally) nausea are common side-effects of failing to properly ground.

There isn't a right or wrong way to cast a circle, but it's important that we use them when weaving magick. Using a circle, whether it is formally cast or instantly willed into being, creates a new sphere; moving energy without one simply pours a small amount of dye into the bowl of water, color that influences the bowl for a moment, but is quickly diluted with the other spheres that come in contact with the water.

CHAPTER TEN

SPELLWORK

Magick is one of the most misunderstood concepts within modern mysticism. New practitioners anticipate that hidden secrets wait to be unveiled and old timers talk about how magick is symbolic and the changes it creates happen within us, not in the greater weave of reality.

Neither is correct - nor is either completely wrong.

Those who have spent some time studying and practicing magick realize that it's a tremendously powerful force for personal change and growth. This is primarily because magick relies on symbolism - which is the same language that our subconscious mind is fluent in and uses to speak to us in dreams, emotions, and intuition. When we deliver our intent using the same language, it only makes sense that our subconscious will hear us and the intended changes will manifest within us.

However, newcomers to magick are also right in anticipating that there is power to change the very nature of reality. Magick is real. It actually works. The major issue we have isn't in ritualistically making magick work, but in understanding the scale on which magick functions and makes changes to reality.

That single word - reality - is key to understanding the full capacity and potential of magick. As practitioners, we don't work our magick in a vacuum but in a tightly woven web of interactions, potential and spirits. The reason that movie magick doesn't work in real life has nothing to do with your lack of belief or your limited ability to raise energy. You can't make like a wizard and throw fireballs across your backyard for one simple reason - you're not working alone.

To create fire, you would need energy. For that fire to exist, for you to hold it in your hand, requires more than your spirit simply being in agreement to engage in the process. The fire itself would need to "agree" to no longer consume energy (in the form of oxygen and a fuel source - for instance, your hand) to keep itself blazing. Several physical laws which allow life to function and interact would have to be suspended. In order to hurl the fire across your backyard, you would have to create some sort of momentum. To throw it like a baseball would require that you reach an agreement with the fire that it would remain cohesive as it flew through the air and that it would change the physical laws that governed its existence, slowing its molecules enough to hold shape while somehow simultaneously keeping them moving quickly enough to remain a flame (which is burning without a fuel source).

It's easy for us to understand the loopholes in natural laws that would have to be found to make this work, but to a magickal practitioner, even that approach is taking the easy way out.

The situation is perhaps easiest to understand through a shaman's eyes.

A shaman believes that all things are alive. In our scenario, a shaman believes that the fire, for instance, is alive and has spirit. While it may not be a sentient being as we understand sentience, it has a purpose and a journey to go through in life. Fire's journey is to consume and then die itself. Light a match and you can watch as the flame slowly works its way down the matchstick, consuming the available material, before it burns itself out. This is Fire's journey. When we summon Fire, such as in the scenario above, we're asking it to suspend its own journey and adhere to our own wishes instead - to become a non-consuming flame until we hurl it at our target.

Under most scenarios, that's not going to happen.

It's not that we lack the necessary power - it's that we lack the necessary reason. What's our reason for asking Fire to suspend its own journey and allow us to throw it across our backyard? For most of us, our reason is simply, "To see if I can do it." That's not a reason. Adopting that approach is much like throwing a rock through a window just to see what happens when we do. Or more accurately, it's like asking a pedestrian if they would kindly stop while we soaked them with a garden hose. Most of the time the answer will simply be, "No," and the pedestrian will continue on their journey.

It's this same concept that comes into play whenever we work magick. Magick works. However, there's a reason why witches don't win the lottery every week. One of the spirits that we have to take into consideration in this scenario is our own spirit. I've been chastised countless times over the decades I've been teaching for being willing to teach spellwork to new students. The argument against doing so is always some variation of, "They'll cause themselves harm if you do." My response has always been, "They won't allow themselves to access that level of power until they're ready for it."

The concepts at play here aren't just a tapestry of relationships - they're also a failsafe. It's easy for us to understand that having a safeguard to keep us from engulfing our backyard in flames is a wise thing to have in place. But what about winning the lottery? What's wrong with being wealthy?

Wealth, from a spiritual perspective, is a beautiful thing when it's applied to the common good. Why? Because whether it's the working of a spell or reaping a financial bounty it's the same tapestry of relationships that are in play. Let's say that I won two hundred million dollars. Hooray for me! Most of us instantly think, "Wow! Here are all of the things I want to do with that money!"

But we forget that we're not working in a vacuum.

There are our friends. Our family. Our Tribe. We are part of a large tapestry of spirits; what happens when our own place in that tapestry shifts so dramatically? It doesn't have to be money, it could be extra time or a bountiful harvest from our garden or even an urge to get pizza. When we work magick - or even when we go about the normal parts of our day - we approach reality as if we're in a vacuum instead of a single thread in a tapestry of spirits. What's more is that everything we manifest, every change we bring about in the world, is itself magick. We don't often think of going shopping as magick, but we're manifesting change each time we do so. We rarely think of reaching out to the people in our world, even if it's just to say hello, but once more we're manifesting change each time we greet someone even with a simple, "Good morning." Each and every moment when we work something in our world that changes what existed in one instant into something new is a form of magick. If all of reality is composed of Spirit, then the seemingly mundane changes we make to that flow are no different from the changes we work in our rites. Understand one, you'll understand the other. Respect and honor one, you'll respect and honor the other. As the old mystical principle reminds us, "As below, so above."

We can't work epic levels of magick because we aren't mindful about the lesser magick that is already at our fingertips. As each of us knows, every step forward on our path is built on the step before it. Let's say we actually learned how to light a candle with our thoughts. We would not be able to advance to holding an unburning flame in our hands until we fully understood, were mindful of, and truly learned to love the candle's flame. This is the spiritual application of love that I speak of - a complete acceptance, understanding, and appreciation of the flame, its journey, and both its light and darkness.

What's more is that we also have to work in harmony, not just with the spirits around us, but with our own spirit and, by extension, our own path. Let's say you're a full time secretary in a small office. Now imagine that your path will only fully manifest the day that you are promoted to project manager and learn the lessons that position holds. Those lessons are critical to where your path will next take you. The promotion will unlock the doors that will lead you to another job that is a synthesis of ability and path - for instance, working with a non-profit that is studying traditional herbal remedies among indigenous peoples. As a secretary, you would never find yourself employed in that role; as a project manager, you're a natural fit. No matter how many lottery tickets you purchase as a secretary, you will never win. It's not because the spirit world is against you - but because it's looking out for you. If you were to win as a secretary, you'd never stick it out in your job, put in the extra hours, and have the opportunity to fill the project manager's shoes when they unexpectedly leave for another company. While things may be challenging in the moment, that journey is necessary to reach the fullness of your path.

The problem with magick is that our perspective is too limited. We don't cross the room and repeatedly run into a wall in an effort to get to the next room, even if the refrigerator is in a directly line from where we're sitting. We walk across the room, we step through doorways, we navigate hallways, and we eventually find what we're looking for in a way that is harmonious with our path and the spiritual environment around us. It's the same way with magick. The shortest line isn't always the path to follow - regardless of whether it's a direction for our path or the outcome of a spell we're working. It's not that we're limited - it's simply that we're not seeing the whole picture.

One of the concepts that we work with on a magickal path is that reality as we perceive it is simply an illusion. Given the perspective we've considered to this point, we could succinctly frame our journey as spiritual beings experiencing physical reality, not physical beings striving for a spiritual experience. The limitations that we encounter in this lifetime - time, space, matter, etc. - are only there because we choose to experience them. Our natural state is a spiritual one. In the larger scheme of our existence, we incarnate into this specific lifetime with all of its physical laws for a very short period of time. Before we incarnate and after we have left this life behind, we are not bound by things such as the walls of our home, the confines of our material form, or even the limitations of linear time.

When a practitioner embarks on a spiritual expedition - such as what is achieved through shamanic journeying - the practitioner doesn't need to travel anywhere since, from a spiritual perspective, distance is simply an illusion. The shaman's spirit doesn't leave their body an empty shell in order to project itself into another place or time. They don't "journey" to another level of reality. The journeying simply involves the removal some of the illusions that construct the shaman's perspective of physical reality - illusions that separate the shaman from the holistic nature of spiritual reality. Once these illusions are removed (a process that includes a great deal of personal work with the practitioner's perceptions, weaknesses and fears), the shaman is capable of seeing beyond the limitations of the illusion to access the energy, wisdom and knowledge that are then revealed. When viewed from the perspective that the only boundaries are those which we perceive to be real, then all things, times, places and events become part of the same integrated spiritual energy.

If this is true, then it holds an interesting implication for our ritual work, regardless of whether those rituals involve celebrations, the honoring of milestones or kindred spirits, or actually focusing our will to a specific end. If all of reality is integrated into a single, holistic spiritual energy, when viewed from a spiritual perspective, our actions and intents become as real as we are. After all, regardless of whether it is ourselves or our actions, the result is simply an expression of the same spiritual energy.

If you will, stretch your mind for a moment and imagine our rites, not as creating an intent and releasing it into the universe, but as giving birth to a spiritual being. This being is extraordinarily limited. Its intent and actions mirror the intent we placed in our rite. This being is only as strong as the energy we put into it. But given the parameters of our rite, it will act on our behalf until it reaches the end of its "life" and is reintegrated into the broader scheme of spiritual reality. It won't have even our limited understanding and perspective to rely on when it encounters multitudes of possible outcomes. This being can only draw upon the original intent we instilled in it.

When viewed from this perspective, it begins to become clear why spellwork is such an inexact art. We aren't shooting a magickal "arrow" at a target; we're essentially training a mystical "toddler" and asking them to carry out a simple task on our behalf and then sending it off on its own. The deeper our rites, the more "training" we can instill in the being we create. But in the end that being is still extraordinarily limited and we are releasing our intent and energy almost blindly into the universe.

I'm not suggesting that we're creating an actual spiritual being. That's a different process altogether and one that, while I was taught the process by one teacher who embraced the concept in her own work, is not something that I've chosen to integrate into my own practice and is not something that I teach. What I'm suggesting is that it may be beneficial to us to look at our rituals from another perspective, one that gives us a clearer idea of how the energy we raise behaves once we release it into the universe. If we think of the implications of our rites as the creation of such a being – rather than the vague concept of releasing our intent into the universe – then we will be able to make more informed choices regarding our actions, rituals, and spellwork and will have a better understanding of how our energy and intent influences the world around us.

We've discussed at length that we're spiritual beings living life from a physical perspective. We've considered the concept that reality is what we manifest and that it's our own belief in the limitations of what we're capable of accomplishing that keeps our magick within very precise boundaries. What we haven't considered is that there are ways to leave both of these restrictions behind.

To fully embrace this journey, we need to begin to shift our perspective. Much of what we've learned about the structure of reality was through our interaction with the boundaries that we agreed (when we came into this incarnation) would be in place to help us grow. We believe that the walls around us are solid, that gravity holds us to the earth, that if you cut us we will bleed.

However, this is an incomplete understanding of what we're experiencing. What we fail to consider is reality from a shaman's perspective.

In shamanism, everything is alive. In all honesty, it's a very straightforward concept, just one that is difficult for us to wrap our minds around. If all of reality is composed of spiritual energy, then that energy must have a spiritual source. The only source for spiritual energy, by default, is the Divine as it transcends all boundaries and limitations. If the book you're holding is composed of the same spiritual energy that you're created from, then by default, the two of you are equally "alive" as both of you are created from the same living spiritual energy.

That doesn't imply that you're equally sentient; just that you're both composed of Spirit.

Think of it in levels of consciousness or, to be more accurate, in the ways that each of us manifests our own reality. You, as a human being, manifest your energy on the world around you in extremely vibrant ways. In a very real sense, you're at the top of the spiritual food chain. You have an immense variety of tools and perceptions at your disposal. Your ability to deductively think, to imagine, to create art - each and every way that you use to consider reality around you also manifests and changes that reality.

An equal spiritual being, say your family dog or cat, is composed of exactly the same spiritual energy that you are composed of. However, because their energy and cognitive processes are different than yours, they have a lessened ability to manifest their reality on the world around them. Instead, they experience the world around them through senses that we lose touch with under the vibrancy of our logical minds. We're distracted with all of the symbolism and concepts of the world around us while they are experiencing a much more instinctive life, one where they frequently respond rather than deduce. We structure reality with our deductive minds; they experience it. But where we tune into the local weather forecast to discover the storm that's brewing over the horizon, they can feel the energy shift and gather. Where we have taught ourselves to respond to the energy that has manifested before us, they live in a world where they instinctively feel that energy beginning to build.

A step farther down the spiritual food chain (for lack of a better term) would be your house plants, your garden, the trees that many practitioners work with. They're alive but it could easily be argued that they have a less vibrant interaction with the energy around us than we do. We don't fully understand how they experience reality, but imagine an existence where you are so in tune to the flow of the seasons, to the cycle of the sun and the moon, that it actually defines your perspective of reality. Just like our beloved family pet, the trees and plants in the world around us are created from the same spiritual energy that forms us, it's just that their perspective - and by extension, their ability to manifest reality - is different from our own.

It's an easy jump for us to make from our existence to that of our faithful animal companion. After all, there are similarities between how they interact with the world and how we do. We both have legs, we both eat, we play together, show each other affection, and we've all watched our pets dream. Our tools for interacting with physical reality have taught us that if it seems similar to us, it probably is similar. If it seems different, it probably is different. However, this is based solely on our ability to perceive the physical manifestation of spiritual energy. It's an ability to see an end product, not the creation of that product. And if we want to truly engage in magick, we need to shift our perception, we need to first understand the entire process, then allow ourselves to participate.

Our family pet? Yes, it's alive. We can see that with our eyes. The tree that grows in a local park? Well, we grudgingly admit that it must be alive as well, although we often toss out caveats to that concept. The computer mouse we used to navigate the Internet? Oh, c'mon... it's a piece of plastic. How in the world can it be alive?

That mouse is composed of spiritual energy, just like our family dog and the herb garden on our apartment windowsill. It's composed of spiritual energy just as we are as human beings. While it seems to completely contradict our logical minds, if everything that is composed of spiritual energy is alive, then even though it obviously experiences reality in a much different way than we do, our food processor, our car, our microwave oven, even our home computer are also alive.

In the movie, The Matrix, one of the characters explained when Neo tried to bend a spoon with his mind, "Do not try to bend the spoon; that's impossible. Instead only try to realize the truth: There is no spoon." That's the flip side of the coin we're considering today. What we need to realize is that, if A) everything is created from spiritual energy, B) everything created from spiritual energy is alive, and C) there is only one source (the Divine) for spiritual energy, then D) we are not only the spoon, but we are also Divine.

The acceptance of this concept is much more important than the applications behind it. Simply allowing ourselves to embrace the reality of our world being alive will open up amazing doorways on its own. There is one part of this concept that applies directly to the concept of why magick doesn't work the way we think it should - yet.

It's pretty easy for us as humans who walk a mystical spiritual path to accept the concept that we manifest reality around us. What we often fail to consider is that so does every other person that we interact with. When we gather with our coven-mates to do ritual work, it isn't one of us that is solely responsible for manifesting reality - we do so together. However, we do the same thing with our co-workers. With our children. With the family pet. With the tree in our backyard.

With the book we're holding in our hands.

We can't magickally turn our dog into a horse or change the color of our car by sheer force of will because these beings are alive and manifesting their own reality. Changing a fir tree into an apple tree would completely subvert the will and experience of the original species. To upgrade our personal computer through force of will alone would be invalidating the worth and experience of our old PC. To do anything of this sort would be to work incredibly dark magick. We would be completely subverting the will of another to fulfill our own selfish desires.

Magick primarily works in the seams between spheres of manifestation. Think back to the concept of spheres we considered a short time ago. Anything we manifest at this level of our work has to slip between the spheres in our reality, not just around the boundaries of our own sphere, but without violating the boundaries of our family pet, our beloved rose bush, or the book we hold in our hands. If you were able to chart the interactions between those subjects, you would find that your abilities manifest in the open spaces between those spheres, not in the face of the flow of another's reality.

That's one of the core reasons why witches, shamans and the type have traditionally worked magick behind closed doors, in the dead of night, or with the first light of sunrise. First of all, with fewer people watching and aware, there are less spheres to work around. Second, even when there are folks watching, our sense of belief (as opposed to a sense of disbelief) is heightened when it's dark. Without all of the visual stimuli to remind us of physical reality, our own grasp on the world we manifest around us begins to relax a little. And with that grip relaxed, we believe that we're capable of doing more when we're cloaked in darkness, shadows, and candlelight than we believe we're capable of when the sun is in the sky overhead.

The next level of this process is to begin to release your hold on your own limitations. If you can completely manifest a new reality for yourself, as long as it doesn't grossly violate the spheres around you, you can do absolutely amazing things.

In one of my favorite books, *Magic and Mystery in Tibet* by Alexandra David-Neel, the author describes people recognizing teachers and students from past lives, routinely surpassing the limitations of the human body, working verifiable magick, and appearing in more than one place at a time. In *Tales of a Shaman's Apprentice*, ethnobotanist Mark Plotkin finds a culture in the Amazon jungle where their entire practice of medicine has been learned from consciously interacting with the spirit world. Quoting a village medicine man, the author was instructed to enter the spirit world through use of a certain hallucinogenic herb and seek out a certain spirit. "He wears a red breechcloth. In one hand he carries a war club; in the other, plants. You must drink more of the *ku-pe-de-vuh* until the demon begins to speak. He will teach you how to cure by singing and by using healing plants. That is all."

The list goes on and on.

At this level of the process, the key is releasing your own expectations and limitations. Both authors listed above speak of transformative experiences that the various practitioners had to undergo in order to accomplish such things. In Ms. David-Neel's book, rituals were undertaken that required a complete surrender of one's sense of self and all attachments to that concept. Using a hallucinogenic short-cut, such as that described in *Shaman's Apprentice*, isn't easier

- or safer. When asked if he could partake in the *ku-pe-de-vuh*, the author was simply told, "'No. This is a very dangerous plant. Many apprentices have taken it and some have lost their minds. Some did not survive.' After a moment's consideration, the shaman then told the author, 'If you take it you will die.'"

Releasing expectations and limitations is not a simple process, primarily because we've used both concepts to define our world from a very early age. While it may seem at first glance that it's a simple matter of "just believing," these limitations are intimately tied into our understanding of who we are. In a very real sense, our limitations are us. Letting go of those limitations isn't simply a matter of personal transformation, but of spiritual evolution.

CHAPTER ELEVEN

THE ELEMENTS

Several years ago, I was in the midst of a shamanic journey, being guided by my spirit teacher in a new method of connecting with the energy we associate with the Elemental power of Earth. My spirit hands had been thrust into the earth, discovering that, even with the soil's ever-present story of life and death, it was only the first level of the energy I sought.

Pushing my spirit self deeper, I found the stones of the earth, the bones of the mountains, the continental plates that moved with such power that their journeys created mountains and earthquakes and sent molten stone exploding into the sky. The energy was intense. Raw. Primal. It was more power than I'd ever sought to wield. But my teacher, knowing what I did not, guided me deeper still.

I plunged deep into the earth, my spirit swimming through molten rock until I reached the Earth's core. There I found the energy that my teacher had guided me to connect with - limitless power, impossible to measure or describe.

A Closer Look At The Elements

One of the key components in working with magic, especially when performing a rite on a spiritual plane, is that the fewer qualifiers you need to grasp any concept, the more cleanly the energy of your rite will flow.

For instance, when I cast a circle and call upon the energy of Earth, I typically visualize either the rich loam of a Northwest old growth forest or the rugged mountain peaks of Alaska. While I can clearly feel the energy of those places and the visualization of a specific location makes it much easier to connect with that energy, I'm also unintentionally limiting the energy by saying, "The energy of Earth in this rite will mirror the energy that I'm currently visualizing." Rather than drawing upon the core of the Element, I've drawn upon an aspect of that Element or, to put it more simply, a single manifestation of its core energy. Mountain peaks and old growth forests contain beautiful energy, but what if the gentle wisdom of a river stone, worn smooth by the passage of water and time, is a better match for my intended outcome? What happens when we call Earth and our filter isn't a location such as an old growth forest, but a direction, a color, or a list of correspondences? Magick, by its very nature, is an odd combination of subtle interactions and precise definitions. Drawing upon specific imagery, labels, or qualities when working with an energetic concept will often ratchet up the available power at our fingertips but at the same time it limits the forms that energy can take. The way that the energy manifests in our world may take on an unexpected form due to the multitude of interactions that the energy faces once we release it, but the manner in which we raise, direct, release and ground that energy will mirror the limitations – implied or intentional – that we place upon it when we summon that energy to us.

It's a little easier to understand the concept if we use the Element of Water to illustrate the challenge before us. A mud puddle, a gentle sprinkle, a mountain lake, a tsunami, the ocean, a downpour, and the driving rain of a hurricane all contain water, but the energy present in each of those concepts feels quite different than any of the other types of energy in that grouping. The reason is that we aren't connecting with the core energy of that Element, but rather the energy that Element manifests as it undertakes its own journey.

Here in my native Oregon, it's an extraordinarily simple matter to connect with the energy of Water. Not only does the Pacific Ocean await to the west, but countless rivers, streams and lakes cover the landscape in the part of the state where I live. And then there's the rain. We get a lot of it out here and large portions of the Northwest are actually classified as a temperate rainforest.

Each aspect of Water that surrounds me doesn't represent the core concept of the Element, but the energy present in a portion of its journey. For instance, by the time the rain falls around me it's already evaporated from the ocean (another type of Water energy) by the heat of the sun (Fire), been carried by the winds and clouds (Air) before falling to the ground (Earth). While the core energy is still very much the Element of Water, it has been joined by other Elemental energies, slightly changing its flavor and flow. In the vast majority of rituals that you will perform, connecting with an Element in this manner will make almost no difference whatsoever in the outcome of your rite. The variation between using energy in this manner and connecting with it in another form is almost imperceptible.

However, things work differently when you're doing spellwork that's intended to have a significant impact or you're working magick on a non-physical level. After all, there is an immense difference in focus, for example, between asking for a generic blessing for your day and seeking healing for a loved one who has been diagnosed with a serious condition. When you're doing intense spellwork or have shifted to one of the more subtle realms (I've found that our labels and definitions are a poor fit for that level of reality, so I tend not to use any), you need to understand that you aren't working on a level of existence where rigid definitions form the landscape, but in a realm that is ruled by symbolism. When viewed from a symbolic perspective, there is a vast difference in energy between the ocean and a pond, between a gentle sprinkling of rain and a driving rainstorm. Certainly they each represent the energy of Water, but the symbolism of each is a completely separate concept.

In order to work around this issue, it's necessary to connect not with a specific manifestation of a type of energy (the ocean, a river, a gentle rain) or an assigned list of qualities and correspondences, but the core concept of that energy.

My current spirit teacher guided me to the understanding that Air is the energy of unity through expansion. It creates a connection between all things by growing to encompass everything that comes within its realm. Don't think of Air as a breeze that caresses the trees, flowers, earth, and yourself as it whispers by on its own journey, but instead consider the atmosphere. While it manifests in an endless variety of ways, the atmosphere expands into every space that is opened to it, halted only by the energy of the other Elements. It's this nature, a unity through the encompassing of all things, that is found at the heart of Air.

On my path, Earth is opposite of Air and represents unity through compression. While trees and plants sink their roots deep into the soil to hold themselves in place, it is the gravity created by our planet that holds all things to it. Soil nurtures life, holding it to the mortal realm. Even earthquakes and volcanoes are produced by tectonic plate movement, two plates compressing together until one of them slips or the growing energy finds a weak point through which it can escape.

I was shown that Fire represents change through release. Science has taught us that, while energy cannot be created nor destroyed, it can be changed from one form to another. Fire is the catalyst for this process. It burns wood to ash and the fires of the sun change ice to water, water to vapor. In each transformation, Fire offers a breaking of bonds, a dramatic and sudden release from one energy construct to something entirely different.

In my practice, Water is the other side of Fire's transformative coin. Where Fire creates change through release, Water creates change through connections. Water wears away the stone, changing stone to sand and carrying each grain of sand to a new relationship as a beach or riverbed. It changes a lifeless desert into a field of flowers, not by destroying the earth and releasing its energy into another form, but by slipping through the soil, reaching the waiting energy of the flowers, and acting as the catalyst that allows the flower's energy to develop a relationship between soil and sun.

When doing intense spellwork or working magick on a more subtle plane, the practitioner's own energy becomes the energy of Spirit, uniting the four Elements and tying your own energy to the rite. There is no clearer illustration that we need to take responsibility for our actions, both on mundane and magical levels, than to realize that we weave ourselves into our rituals and magick.

CONNECTING WITH THE ELEMENT OF AIR

The typical approach to learning the Elements (Air, Fire, Water, Earth, and Spirit) is to sit down with a table of correspondences and start memorizing. Each Element is said to have a corresponding color, corresponding qualities, and specific things that it's used for. We memorize those correspondences and then begin learning how each Element - and only that Element - is suited to various types of rituals and spellwork.

Yeah... we're not going to do any of that.

In fact, we're going to take a completely different approach.

Say the word, "Air," out loud. You can whisper it, sing it, shout it - just make the sound. Did you hear that? That's Air.

Now blow a breath through your lips like you were blowing out the candles on a birthday cake. That's Air.

Knock three times on whatever hard surface you're near. That sound? You guessed it - Air.

Stop and think about where you might go to find Air - now stop thinking! That thought. It's Air.

Step outside for a moment and feel the breeze. Don't worry - the rest of this lesson will wait. You're back? That's Air. Now feel the still space around you. Also Air.

Every sound, every thought, the caress of the wind or the stillness around you - it's all Air. When we call upon the Element of Air in our rites, we aren't calling upon correspondences we've memorized from a list; we're calling on the very fabric of reality. In my opinion, we don't need to memorize - we need to connect.

CONNECTING WITH THE ELEMENT OF FIRE

Simply put, Fire is power. In my opinion, it is the easiest Element to connect with and the most challenging to understand and work with in a rite.

The reason for this is that Fire's journey is intimately tied to our understanding and ability to embrace our own personal power. As human beings, we tend to find a comfortable space in which to stay and work. We rarely push our boundaries. In all honesty, most of us prefer not to work outside of our "comfort zone."

Imagine Fire as a warm, crackling presence in a fireplace on a cold winter's day. Now imagine that you're sitting on the fireplace hearth, inches from the flame. You can stay there for a moment or two until it becomes too warm to take any longer.

At its heart, Fire's journey is about working with an active, powerful force and learning when, where, how, and why to apply that force. It's the process of connecting with something wild and out of control and learning, not to tame it, but to consciously apply it in a controlled manner.

Take, for instance, anger.

I have heard countless spiritual practitioners over the years utter some version of, "You shouldn't get angry," or, "Anger is bad," yet neither is true. Both perspectives are really saying, "Anger is powerful and scares me." Anger is an energetic tool. When we feel threatened - emotionally or physically - anger is a pool of additional energy, strength, and will that suddenly opens to us. It's inappropriate for us to throw another person headfirst into the pool and push them under, but it's completely appropriate for us to take a glass, dip it into those waters, and consciously drink deeply in order to summon additional energy and face a challenging situation.

Fire is symbolic of any intense energy - including emotion. The thing that distinguishes the intensity of Fire from the intensity of any other emotion is that Fire consumes. It wraps itself around the fuel it's given, breaks down that fuel, and changes it back into pure energy. When left to run wild, it can consume an entire landscape; when controlled, it can be warmth and light in the middle of a dark forest.

Calling Fire into a rite is opening oneself to power, inviting that power to join you in its own way, and then setting the boundaries for that power much like you set stones around a campfire. Fire is unchained potential, harnessed and directed. And that's really Fire's secret. Fire is like a powerful horse that takes willingly to the reins. It's like capturing a tsunami in your hands and realizing that it is truly content to simply be held until you unleash it. It's rage that is transformed by a kind word, passion that opens secret doors with a lover, and fire that can be used to warm and create when controlled or destroy everything in sight when left unchecked.

If you think about it, we're like that as well. Left unchecked, we destroy the world around us, we harm each other, and we wreak havoc as far as the eye can see. Control and direct that same spirit and we create beauty, nurture life, and the world thrives in our care.

CONNECTING WITH THE ELEMENT OF WATER

Being a Pisces, I'm rather biased about the Element of Water. For me, it's easy to understand and one of the Elements I work with the most, especially when you consider that the Pacific Ocean is less than an hour from my front door. Whether it's rain or snow, a mountain river or pristine lake, morning fog, or the Pacific itself, my native Northwest has Water in abundance.

One of the key aspects that we have yet to explore in that article is another application of Water's ability to "change through connections."

For argument's sake, let's separate reality into defined levels. In our example (setting aside our understanding that "All is One") we stand here in the physical embracing the illusion that we're separated from the spiritual. How do we "connect" to the spirit world and "change" our position from here to there?

Simple. We use Water.

Whether it's a long bath to soak our worries away or a shower to wash away the energy that clings to us, whether we're soaking in the tub or soaking up the heat of the shower, we all instinctively know that Water has the ability to move us from one state of being to the next. Because of the nature of symbolism, Water not only represents the ability to connect but depending on your perspective, can either represent the vehicle by which we connect or the boundary between where we are and where we want to reach.

Consider the practice of water magick in our world. At its heart, water magick involves filling a bowl or cauldron with water and seeing the surface of the water as the boundary between our world and the next. We literally push the intent for our rite across that barrier and release it on the other side of the boundary between the two worlds (represented by the surface of the water) to highly empower our rite. This is seeing Water's connective ability as a barrier that can be easily crossed.

The other way of looking at Water is as the connection by which we can create change - in other words, empowering ourselves to be that change. If you ever have the opportunity to sit in on a class that I teach in person, you may notice that I drink water during class. This seems like an obvious thing for a speaker to do, but each time I take a drink, I'm consciously taking Water's "change through connections" inside of me and allowing myself to be changed into the tool that benefits those gathered in class.

CONNECTING WITH THE ELEMENT OF EARTH

Most of us who call upon the power of Earth do so as a source of energy. We sink our symbolic roots deep into the "soil," reconnect, and pull life up into us from the energy of the planet itself.

We see Earth as slow. It's challenging for us to perceive with our naked eyes the process of a mountain eroding or a glacier moving across the landscape. With this in mind, you might be surprised to learn that one of the ways I work with the energy of Earth is when a major, fundamental shift needs to quickly happen in my path.

On my path, Earth is opposite of Air and represents unity through compression. While trees and plants sink their roots deep into the soil to hold themselves in place, it is the gravity created by our planet that holds all things to it. Soil nurtures life, holding it to the mortal realm. Even earthquakes and volcanoes are produced by tectonic plate movement, two plates compressing together until one of them slips or the growing energy finds a weak point through which it can escape.

When the pressure in our own path seems to be building past the point we can handle, the energy of Earth can release that pressure. Like a tectonic plate that is pressing against another, we can use Earth's energy to "slip" beyond what's obstructing us.

But that's not Earth's secret.

Earth reminds us that no matter what happens, life goes on. In the aftermath of a massive earthquake, plants continue to grow, animals return to forage or hunt, and birds take to wing once more. We stand there in the rubble, amazed that it wasn't the end of everything. Earth teaches us that at the core of the changes that come on our path is the word "change." Nothing remains the same. Everything changes. Rewind geological time and it's likely that the place you're standing now was once covered in ice. Rewind a bit farther and you'd find yourself at the bottom of a tropical ocean without moving an inch. Everything changes, everything evolves, but life still goes on.

With all of the craziness that's happening in the world around us, with all of the news stories that reflect the threats that are present to us and our way of life, it's easy to get lost in the moment. Whether it's a challenging personal situation or something on a much larger scale, Earth reminds us that it's just a moment in the timeline of life. This too shall pass. No matter how hard the winds may blow, if we simply sink our roots deep into Earth, we shall still be standing when the challenging moment has passed.

Earth teaches us scale. Where Fire exists only as long as there is fuel to burn, Earth continues on beyond the limits of our comprehension. Earth teaches us that our strength is in our roots - the place where we draw inspiration, life, and sustenance - not in the debris that the winds may carry. Earth teaches us that whatever trials we may be facing, they will pass and the birds will still sing, the animals forage and hunt, and the seasons continue to turn.

CHAPTER TWELVE

MAGICKAL ATTRIBUTES

Shadows danced along the walls of the tiny hut, even as those gathered within sat motionless around the crackling fire. The woman who had called them together smiled; her eyes were bright and dancing like a child's, her hands gentle like a mother's touch, and her face creased with the lines of a crone's wisdom. Pulling a cloth-wrapped bundle from beneath her warm cloak, she slowly unwrapped it to reveal the contents it had hidden.

In her hands lay a round, uneven stone, about the size of a small peach. The stone was the same color as the fruit it mirrored, but a soft yellow glow ebbed and flowed within it, the shadows of the crone's wrinkled face lengthening and fading in response.

"This came to me," she said quietly, her voice still and strong, carry the strength of a much younger woman. "Tell me about it."

She handed the stone to the person sitting to her left.

"It's warm," the man whispered in unexpected awe, his eyes fixed on the stone he held. "It's as if it's alive."

Almost reluctantly, he passed it on to the woman sitting next in the circle.

A look of surprise wrinkled the women's forehead, her questioning eyes turning to the man who had already spoken. "To me," she offered, shaking her head slowly as she offered her differing perspective, "it feels cold - like the ocean surf."

She passed it on. "It's soft," the next person said. "I can squeeze it and it gives beneath my hands, like a ripe fruit."

"No it doesn't," the next person contradicted as it was their turn to experience the stone. "It's hard. I've never felt anything so solid."

From hand to hand the stone traveled, each person experiencing something completely unique when they held the rock.

At last it returned to the old woman's hands.

"What does it mean?" one of those gathered around the fire asked. "How can it be warm and cold, soft and solid? It can't be all those things. It doesn't make any sense."

"But it does," the crone countered as she wrapped the stone in its cloth once more, returning the bundle to the folds of her cloak. "The stone is magick. Magick isn't a thing. It's a connection. Each of you whom I invited here, you are each unique. No one else experiences the same thing that you do when you hold the stone. You're brave enough to speak, to share, and to grow. Magick isn't a stagnant thing that you can define. It changes constantly, each time someone interacts with it. If all you were capable of doing do is memorizing what I told you it means, then I wouldn't have invited you here."

The old woman smiled as if to reassure the gathered men and women who leaned forward, listening to her wisdom.

"You've gathered here, at this fire, because you seek knowledge. If I simply wrote it down, tomorrow it would be out of date. We gather around the fire because the flames flicker and the wood is consumed. In time, the warmth will fade to cold ash. Only by renewing the fire, by adding new wood, can it continue to burn. Wisdom is like that. So is magick. If you don't add to it, it fades. Your calling isn't simply to learn what I have to teach, but to add to the fire we build together."

OOO

It seemed a little too easy to say that, while correspondences have their place and that, while an elementary understanding of how qualities and attributes are symbolically assigned is useful, it's ultimately a dead end. In all honesty, it doesn't matter what the books say or what you can memorize from a chart. What is important is how you connect with symbolism, concepts, and traditions.

Each thing we consider in magick has a hidden lesson. If we learn that red symbolizes the Element of Fire, what have we truly learned? What we need to do is to spend some time with a candle, watching the flame flicker and dance. We need to feel the warmth of the flame, watch the wax melt, and understand why we are careful to keep the flame carefully tamed. Each step in that process teaches us much about ourselves, about others, about Nature, about magick, and about the weave of reality. After all, as we've considered in some depth together, "All is One."

What's more is that our unique connection - the way we experience "the stone" - is not because there is one way to connect with such an object, but because it is a reflection of our own sacred nature and how our core self connects with magick. We experience that connection differently simply because we each have a different calling. A warrior will not experience "the stone" the same way that a healer will experience it. An herbalist's connection will be much different than that of a diviner.

Remember, this is a quest - not a test. This path is about a journey, not about a destination or finding the correct answers. Only by allowing yourself to explore and find your own symbolism can you add your own wood to magick's fire. By embracing the perspective and vision of other practitioners, no matter how new or experienced that person may be, you allow them to add their own fuel to the flame. Together, we can rekindle that fire and share it, candle to candle, soul to soul, and by the light of that shared flame, we will illuminate hidden secrets to embrace and explore.

NUMBERS

Numbers are a necessary, yet challenging, concept to incorporate into our magickal workings. As we considered earlier when we looked at the concept of Levels, symbolism is the language of magick and exists on Level Two; numbers are a linear concept and call Level One their home. So how do we take a rigid and defined concept like numbers and work it into our magick?

There are two ways to teach the symbolism of numbers. The first way is pretty common. You make a list of numbers and offer what they correspond to. When I take this approach, I like to put them in a simple poem.

> One is yourself, higher and true
> Dark God and light God, counted as Two
> Three is the Goddess, young, middle, old
> Four quarters are called, our rite they do hold
> Five Elements there are (to Sprit's a nod)
> Six, although even, is counted as odd
> Seven is lucky, though no one knows why
> Eight Sabbats do follow the sun through the sky
> Nine feet the circle (it's three times three)
> Ten is for math, (ugh! Someone save me!)
> Eleven vibrates, especially when doubled
> Twelve leaves one out, magick is troubled
> Thirteen moons there are in a year
> Remember these numbers, their meanings so "clear"

Why a poem? Mostly because I'm really bad at remembering things. Every time Crow grabs my attention, for instance, I have to say the poem about using crows as divination to find the meaning.

One is for sorrow
Two is for mirth
Three is a wedding
Four is a birth
Five is for silver
Six is for gold
Seven a secret never is told

I'm not kidding. For me it's like counting on my fingers. I've been doing this for countless years and still go through the poem each and every time I encounter Crow. The only piece I remember off hand is the number two, mostly because my shamanic working name is Two Crows.

And that is the easy way of working with the symbolism of numbers.

The hard way is kind of like working with Runes (a practice in its own rite that we will not be exploring in any depth in this book). To really understand the concept, you have to sort of crack your brain in half, rearrange the pieces, and then put it back together. Nothing rigid (like a number or a Rune) should, by all reasoning, refer to the flow of reality.

And yet both Runes and numbers do.

The number one is reasonably easy to understand, simply because it stands alone. It's not simply the number one, but any sort of symbolism associated with isolation. (While many of us have negative connotations with words like "isolation" it can be a very positive concept, like meditating within yourself to center and clear your mind. Or take the concept of "All is One" – while it is singular, it is also all-encompassing; there is nothing outside of that concept.)

Two is a partnership of any sort, whether it's an intimate union or duality of two opposing forces. Both of those are pretty clear. What's useful about both one and two in magickal work is that they function at an immediate level. One is typically your perspective. Two is typically your perspective joined by that of another. Pretty straightforward so far.

We typically associated the number three with the Goddess as she has three phases (Maiden, Mother, Crone). That's easy enough to understand. We also take a step beyond that and say, "Three is a pattern." It's one of the key reasons why spoken phrases in spellwork are uttered three times. ("Once is an anomaly; twice a coincidence; three times is a pattern.") To take things a step farther, patterns (symbolized by the number three) provide an energetic template for the flow of reality. Think of it as offering a paint-by-numbers picture at arm's length to a palette of intelligent, movable, sentient ink. The ink will color the picture, but it may not end up exactly the way you imagined. It's why we work with the number three in spellwork - it creates that pattern.

Then things begin to get tricky. Numbers in magick and ritual work are like a ladder. The higher rung you stand on to work your rite, the deeper into magick you delve. While it's a field of study in its own right, the symbolism of numbers in magick tends to be linked in pairs: one and two; three and four; and so on. Each pair takes you to a deeper level of magick. One and two, for instance, are very immediate workings. Three and four are energetic structures. Five and six are bridges that connect "below" and "above."

For example, many pagans typically cast a circle by calling in four Elements. Four is like three, creating a template, but one that has little to no flexibility. This creates a very stable energetic platform to work with when casting a circle but, when used to work a spell, typically seeks a result with either an overwhelming success or a total failure - there's very little middle ground with four. (Which is why most practitioners use the symbolism of three when working a spell instead of the number four. We'd typically rather have a lesser result than risk having none at all.)

If we call five Elements (Spirit is typically considered the fifth Element), we build an energetic bridge between our circle and a higher level of reality (typically the spirit world as represented by symbolism we associate with the Goddess and the God within the rite, but there are countless other ways to focus such energy.) Using five in spellwork is tricky as you're throwing the door wide open for spirits who are interested in bending reality to their will - which is what we do in spellwork. It's one of the reasons why it's critical to develop relationships and invite spiritual allies, rather than simply command spirits and expect them to submit to your will.

Calling in six Elements establishes a very firm circle that is rooted in both physical and multidimensional space. (Generally "above" and "below" are used in such a rite.) This is a much safer way to work a spell (using six in the bending) as it limits the spirits to those that will assist with the specifically intended outcome of the spell. Like four, six also carries a much greater risk of simply doing nothing - or hitting it out of the park, grand slam home run. As an example of the use of the number six in a rite, you could invite the Elements (four), Spirit (five), and ancestral spirits (six) or a spirit guide or even an intentional and defined incorporation of your own energy and spirit into the rite.

The numbers continue to pair from this point forward, the "odd" number offering a greater (if unpredictable) chance of success with the "even" number offering more stability but restricting (and perhaps preventing) certain outcomes. Each additional pair steps farther away from mundane reality and becomes harder and harder to explain short of leading you through guided meditations to embrace the concepts. Seven and eight are tricky to work with as much of what you're influencing steps beyond the concept of linear time and begins working with what is easiest (if incredibly inaccurate) to explain as a "multi-incarnation perspective." I've worked with nine, but not ten. Nine works from an "All is One" perspective and actually requires you to fully release your individual identity to work with the magick it symbolizes. I can sort of feel the concept of ten but I run into energetic contradictions working with the concepts of ten that snap me out of the frame of mind needed to work with it every time I run into them.

To offer some perspective, each pair of numbers symbolizes energetic reality, much like the numbers one and two. With one person (an odd number), you have freedom to simply go. With two people (an even number), you have both assistance and restriction. That concept is somewhat challenging for us to understand just in our relationships. (Example: Suzy will help me with this, but even though she's not asking for it, anticipates that I'll help her in return with something else. Furthermore, I know she'll want to steer things this way, so I'm not going to be able to do everything I want with it if she's helping.)

Each pair of numbers - as applied to magickal workings - takes us a step deeper into the mysteries. Almost all of modern magick can be found between the numbers one and five. To give you an idea of how much we have yet to explore, I was taught the concepts up to twenty-one by a truly amazing instructor; even my teacher couldn't grasp its counterpart in twenty-two.

SHAPES

We're going to approach the concept of shapes in a slightly different manner than you may have expected. (Of course, at this point in our journey together, what has really been presented as expected?) Instead of providing a list of shapes so you can memorize their mystical properties, we're going to learn how to think about shapes from a magickal and ritualistic perspective.

When we looked at the mystical application of numbers, we considered the concept that numbers function on multiple levels of reality when we use them in ritual work. For instance, we may cast a circle by summoning in four Elements, but will work our actual rite using patterns of three.

Shapes work in a similar manner. Whenever we work with a shape in ritual work, there are two things we have to consider: the number of sides in the shape and the patterns which energy will follow as it flows around the interior of that shape.

For instance, let's say we cast a circle to use as a platform to work a spell. There are three different numbers we need to consider in this process: one, four, and three. One is the number of sides that compose a circle. Four represents the Elements we call. Three denotes the pattern we work into the spell.

Each corner (the intersection of sides) in a shape changes the flow of energy. As we considered earlier, it's one of the key reasons why we typically use a circle (or sphere) in our rites. There are no corners to influence the flow of energy, so the energy manifests without further influence from the shape of our sacred space. Sacred space is almost always in a circle for this reason. It has no beginning and no end. If you think of energy as constantly moving, once it begins moving around the circumference of your circle, it does so without interference.

I'll sometimes explain it to students like this. "Let's say, when you face East and call the Element of Air, that it responds by hurling a Super Ball of Air at you. You duck and the super ball flies over your head and hits the inside wall of your circle. Now, since this is magick, the super ball never loses momentum. Your circle/sphere is made of very special material that draws the super ball to it so that it hugs the curve of the circle/sphere's wall. Pretty soon the super ball of Air is zipping around you in perfect circles as it follows the shape (the circle) that your created."

When we use a circle to define our sacred space, we can simply call the energy in and it flows around us. While it's rarely taught (and often inaccurately portrayed), the Elements add their energy and symbolism to our rite by forming a perimeter around our working, our actual ritual taking place within that perimeter circle. The easiest way to understand this concept is to imagine that the Elements (or Quarters as they are often called) form a circular shell around the rite. The rite itself takes place within this shell but the energy of the shell radiates into the rite in much the same way that light or heat radiates so that we can interact with it. It is generally understood that the circle is actually a sphere, but the reasons why it works in this manner are directly tied to the fact that the physical reality we experience is an illusion. Without the illusionary restriction that requires one thing to be in one place at a time, we can form a circular perimeter by calling the Elements and, unrestrained by the illusionary limitations we typically experience, they are in multiple places at one time, forming a sphere instead of just a perimeter circle.

Other sacred shapes require different approaches. For instance, when I work in a sacred square I erect Elemental walls drawing Air down from the atmosphere, Fire from the candle flame, Water from the cauldron, and Earth from the ground below. As we considered earlier, "Four is like three, creating a template, but one that has little to no flexibility. This creates a very stable energetic platform to work with when casting a circle but, when used to work a spell, typically seeks a result with either an overwhelming success or a total failure - there's very little middle ground with four." However, if you need to erect a barrier to do work in, four - with its stability - can be a useful number to apply to sacred space.

One of the keys to remember is that even though you're working within a different sacred shape (a square instead of a circle, for instance) that all of the change you're manifesting still needs to happen within a circle. It's the concept of spheres of reality. This gets highly complicated very quickly, but here's the easiest illustration of the concept.

When we looked at the symbolism of numbers, we considered that each pair of numbers carried us deeper into magick. This way of thinking of two different things at the same time within the same concept (the symbolism of the number and where it carries us) is critical to understanding deeper magick. To extend this concept, while we cast a circle, we almost never work magick by interacting with the perimeter of the circle itself. Almost without exception, it simply defines our sacred space - but our sacred shape is also more than just a definition of space.

We previously considered that from a shaman's perspective, everything is alive as it is composed of sacred energy, a facet of the Divine. This means that, from certain perspectives, our circle itself is a magickal being. It's useful to stop thinking of your cast circle as a physical space and start thinking of it as an energetic entity or collection of energetic entities who are working together in unison.

It's one of the reasons why I tend to use very clear visualization in my rites when calling the Elemental Quarters. When casting a circle, the Elements all flow together; when casting a square, each takes up its position on its own side of the sacred shape and essentially joins energetic hands to enclose the rite and close the circuit so that their combined energy flows around the sacred shape. Once again, the easiest way to understand this perspective is to stop thinking of your circle as an energetic room and begin considering it as the formation taken up by a group of energetic allies (typically the Elements) that come when you call them to join in your rite.

The dual thinking that is required in this concept is that there are two parts to any rite: the creation of sacred space and the ritual itself. Regardless of the symbolism, numbers, or shapes that we use, the ritual takes place within the same circle in each and every rite: our reality sphere. (When we work a magickal rite with another person or persons, our spheres simply merge into a single, larger sphere for the duration of the rite.) This duality in a magickal working is one of the key reasons why our energy is always connected to a rite: there's simply no way to completely sever ourselves from the working. When we're working with a circle (our reality sphere) within a circle (our cast sacred shape), we don't think of the duality that is in play as the shapes are similar and we aren't typically aware of their distinctiveness. However, it's no different from working with a circle (our reality sphere) inside of any other sacred shape (such as a cast square). This is advanced magick, rarely taught, and requires a great deal of control regarding the flow of energy within a rite as well as specific symbolism where the casting of the sacred shape is concerned.

This duality is also the reason why there is a boundary to a circle which needs to be opened and closed if a practitioner should need to enter or leave in mid-rite. It's this same duality that allows a child or animal to safely cross without interrupting the ritual. Those of us who are experienced in circle work have extensively worked with this very concept of dual ritual structures without even realizing it.

Depending on the work that you're doing, you can stretch your circle into a cone with a point at the top. In this practice, you leave the circular bottom half of the sphere in place (or you turn the whole thing on its head). When the cone points up, you can work with afterlife energies; pointed downward, and you can work with the underworld. (Neither is good nor bad, much like the light and shadow portions of ourselves.) The cone directs the energy to and from the center of the rite - either yourself or a focus item (like a cauldron or altar.)

Much like working with higher numbers, working with shapes with an increasingly larger numbers of sides requires an intense amount of focus. For instance, if you wanted to work a spell that would take play out over the course of one year, you could cast an octagon instead of a circle. Each of the eight sides would correspond to one of the eight Sabbats. To use this approach, it's necessary to have already established a deep connection to (and awareness of) the flow of Nature throughout the Sabbats. It's the energetic signature of each Sabbat that you call upon, one for each of the eight sides, instead of calling upon Elemental energy. I use walls, much like in a sacred square, and form either the top or the bottom into a cone (depending on my intent.)

For simply practical purposes, you will almost never have need to use anything beyond a simple shape. In magickal work, a circle is used nearly 100% of the time. Any other shape is used on rare occasions by adept practitioners who are seeking very specific outcomes to their rite.

Color

If you've wandered down certain Neo-Pagan paths, you've likely encountered the symbolism associated with color. Many new Wiccans, for example, are taught that each color is associated with a direction and an Element. (Or that a direction is associated with an Element and a color. Or that... Well, you get the idea.) For instance, the color yellow is typically associated with the Element of Air and the direction East; red represents Fire and South; blue symbolizes Water and West; green corresponds to Earth and North.

Having a defined system is great when working with a coven, circle or within an established Tradition. It's tremendously useful to have individuals on the same page when working group rituals together. However, the strength in this approach is also its weakness.

When I lay on my back and look at the summer sky, why is the blue I see associated with Water and not Air? If purple is created by mixing the colors blue and red, does that mean it represents the combining of Fire and Water as steam? Are yellow flowers associated with Air instead of the Earth they grow in? I can make the leap to say that red blood represents Fire (the "fire of life" and the "fire of passion") but what about ripe strawberries or the juicy flesh of a watermelon?

While offering focus and direction on a defined path, the concept of predefined correspondences begins to rapidly fall apart when you attempt to apply the symbolism across a wider range than a carefully constructed rite.

What I do when I teach students the concepts of symbolism and color is to have them think about things that, for instance, are yellow. Rather than representing Air, yellow represents dandelions, butter, and the sun. The question then becomes, "What do these things have in common for you?" In the path that I teach, color is only loosely connected to an Element. The deeper bond between the color and the practitioner is found in experience. If we have experienced something, we have a much easier time summoning its energy. Imagine for a moment, what it's like to eat really good chocolate. Seriously. Stop and imagine the chocolate melting on your tongue. Savor the memory of the flavor. Now imagine for a moment what it's like to eat freshly grilled kangaroo. There's an entire energetic process that comes to life when it's something that we have experienced firsthand that simply doesn't occur with a merely intellectual concept.

One of the things that this approach does is tear down walls we didn't know were even present. For instance, let's imagine that you were drawing a candle flame with crayons and paper. A good percentage of us would draw the flame with the color yellow (which traditionally represents Air), not the color red (which is most commonly associated with Fire). Why wouldn't you go with what's already a part of our instinct and intuition even if your correspondence between color and Element is traditionally incorrect?

You might think that this muddies up the energetic landscape to the point that color can't be used in ritual work. For instance, if we all agree that yellow represents Air, when presented with that color in ritual work, our thoughts all uniformly jump to the Element of Air. That's a pretty clean process and is incredibly useful when regularly working magick with the same group of people. So, wouldn't allowing free-form associations just screw things up, even if you practice magick on your own? I find that the opposite is true. Instead of muddying things, it gives us greater energetic depth when working on our own individual path. Instead of simply calling upon Air, I can call upon any of its aspects - stillness, a refreshing breeze, or a strong wind to blow things away. When I use the color yellow in my work, it can represent Air, light, the strength of a lioness, or the richness of butter. In this approach what matters is my intent. The tool that I use is my ability to energetically connect with a chosen concept rather than intellectually remembering a connection.

If you find yourself working with colors on your path, take a moment and ask yourself, "What does this color mean to me?" You may find that your color associations are much more diverse than the traditional correspondences. Rather than confusing your approach to ritual work, having a broader palette of color associations can empower and add some much needed flexibility to your personal approach to magick.

DIRECTIONS

Many modern practitioners call Elemental energy from each of the directions when they cast a circle. The most widely practiced form of this tradition is to call Air from the East, Fire from the South, Water from the West, and Earth from the North. Many practitioners also add Spirit as a "fifth Element," sometimes calling it "from Within and Without," sometimes calling it from "Above and Below," sometimes asking specific gods and goddesses to join in their right, and sometimes (whew!) simply representing Spirit themselves.

I was taught that the directional correspondences for each Element were developed in the United Kingdom. Winds blew off the European continent to the east, connecting the practitioners' thoughts to Air. The equator and warmer climates were to the south, instantly associating that direction with warmth and Fire. The Atlantic Ocean lay to the west, establishing Water in that direction. And the endless ice appearing to the eye as Earth, lay to the north.

Those are extremely useful correspondences - if you're practicing magick in the United Kingdom. But what about the rest of us? What about my students in Australia, where even the seasons are reversed compared to a mystical seeker used to practicing in the Northern Hemisphere? How do we find something that works for us in the place where we live?

What I did – and I encourage you to do the same – is to begin thinking about the environment you live in and the manner in which you subconsciously think of each direction. Perhaps you live in Kansas and there isn't a large body of water to connect with. Which natural body of water do you think of when you think of Water? Perhaps you lived elsewhere as a child near the shores of a majestic lake. Does it make sense to associate Water with the direction in which the lake is found, rather than simply associating the element with a direction?

My own Tradition coincidentally mirrors the correspondences from the United Kingdom. I say coincidentally, because I had discovered my own home for the Elements long before I learned of the associations that many modern practitioners draw upon.

Living in the Pacific Northwest, Water was the easiest element for me to establish a home for. The mighty Pacific Ocean, with all her moods, lay immediately to the west of me. I spent a great deal of my childhood living on her coasts and in my adulthood I return to her again and again. Our natural cycle of precipitation begins in her womb, the rains rising from the sea and moving inland. Each river, each stream in the land I know as home races back to her embrace. All of these added to my placing Water in the west in my own Tradition.

South has always been connected with warmth and heat to me. The farther south you drive from my home, the closer to the equator you draw and the warmer it gets. Southern California and the tropics both lay to the south of me, as is the incredible heat of California's Death Valley and the deserts of the American Southwest. When I think of anything to the south of me, it's always warmer. So South became the home of Fire.

Massive mountains and countless miles of untamed wilderness lay north of me. Washington's Olympic Peninsula; Alaska's Mt. McKinley; the Canadian wilderness; all of these are found to the north. Mountains and thousands of miles of forests, drawing up the energy of the earth. North has always symbolized Earth to me.

Which left Air in the East. Eastern Oregon and Washington are filled with wide open spaces where the winds race unhampered by tree or mountain. There are vast open spaces, rolling plateaus where the wind dances through the grasses, where antelope graze, where your eyes can stretch to the horizon unhindered. There is a certain majesty to the openness, to the wind that blows through your hair, to the endless sky above. Each of these are things I associate with the element of Air, and this Element naturally found its home for me in the East.

I was taught by a Native American woman, whom I studied with for some time, that Spirit is everywhere, that it connects all things. I came to believe, both through her teachings and my own discoveries, that the energy that connects all of us, that gives every living thing substance and life, is one energy, that we all are expressions from the same Source. So when I call upon Spirit, I call it from everywhere, both from within and from without.

As you've probably figured out by now, I'm a big believer in finding your own correspondences to things. Many of the things I teach have evolved and been refined over the last two decades, but the emphasis I place on finding your own path has remained constant. Today, I see calling the Elements from specific directions to be a useful tool, but just a tool. Even I don't consistently call upon them in my rites, just as you wouldn't use a hammer to address every household repair. (Remember, when casting an octagon, I call the energy of each of the Sabbats, rather than calling Elements to form the perimeter sacred shape of the rite.)

Always remember that it doesn't matter what is written in a book; the method that someone else tells you is the "right way" may not be the right way for you. Even rigid concepts, like numbers, are that way only because of their agreed upon meaning within our culture. As I like to tell students, "If it doesn't work for you, it doesn't work (for you)." Explore. Try out ideas from other people and other cultures, but know that the best way is the one you try that you connect with and that empowers your magick and rites. Your practice is uniquely your own. "Your heart is your map and your intuition your compass. Follow them. They will not lead you astray."

CHAPTER THIRTEEN

THE SUN AND THE MOON

It was a clear summer night, the full moon hanging like a rich, ripe fruit in the starry sky. Our coven's ritual had just ended; all of us were hot and panting from another enthusiastic spiral dance, led by one of our younger members. I wandered off alone, sitting in the midst of a nearby field while the rest of the coven talked and milled about, exchanging stories of the previous week and making plans for the coming days.

There, in the darkness, sitting alone in the grassy field, I gazed upon the face of Luna and wondered what my ancestors thought and felt when they gazed up at the same sky. One by one, my coven-mates came and joined me and we talked about the past, about the legacy our ancestors had left us. Did those who came before us realize that the moon was a satellite orbiting the earth we live on? Or was our moon simply a constant companion whose light ebbed and flowed, setting the lunar month? We talked about what each of us would feel if, unfettered by the words of science, we stared up at the moon with a mystical awe. How would we feel simply knowing it as a soft light in our night sky, whose phases mirrored the cycle of growth we saw in the Goddess?

It wasn't a book we were learning from, or even a physical teacher. We learned from the moon itself, from the energy that permeated the air from our circle and spiral dance. It was the whispered voices of our ancestors who spoke to us, as our minds let go of the bonds of time and slipped back through the centuries to earlier rituals.

And for the first time, as we lay in the open field, gazing up at the light of the full moon, I didn't just know what the moon meant. I understood.

One of the concepts that becomes increasingly evident to us as we step ever deeper into the realm of magick is that All is One. At first glance, it may seem to have limited usefulness outside of a touchy-feely perspective for spiritual growth, but that's only because we don't understand the nature of magick.

Imagine that each time you worked a spell, a rune-engraved wooden doorway appeared before you. You'd step through the portal to find yourself in the midst of a mystical landscape. Each action that you carried out there was not only symbolic in nature, but dramatically influenced events in the mundane realm.

Let's say that you had been struggling with your path. It seemed as if there was something blocking your progress. In reality, it may have been a past hurt that still needed to heal or a subconscious hesitancy to proceed down this particular road. However, in this mystical realm, the obstacle appears as a gigantic boulder that has come to rest in the middle of your path.

Simply pushing it out of the way is beyond the limits of your strength. It's clear that you need help, so you step back through the portal, into your sacred space, and begin to work a spell to aid you on the other side of the portal. As you call the Element of Air into your rite, winds begin to push at the rock; Earth causes the ground below it to crumble away and slant downward in the direction you want to move the boulder.

If it is true that All is One, then each time we work magick, we aren't simply moving pieces around on a mystical chessboard until they're positioned as we desire. Each element that we add to our rite - whether it is one of the Elements, a phase of the moon, a symbolic object, the time of year, or even the location where we perform the ritual - *adds itself* to the magick we're working.

Metaphorically speaking, instead of facing the gigantic boulder alone, we find ourselves with Elemental helpers, with animated shovels (since we used one symbolically in our rite), and even the gravitational pull of the moon and sun working to move the boulder.

This is one of the numerous practical reasons why it's so important live in an ethical manner if you choose to walk a magickal path. Not only is all of reality connected ("All is One") but there is a direct correlation between the gratitude and thankfulness you show the various people, spirits, and things that compose your world and the amount of magickal might that you have at your fingertips when you work a rite.

Because of the concept "All is One," anything and everything that exists in our personal reality can be used in a magickal rite. What is important is that we connect with the object and are able to draw upon the symbolism it inherently holds.

Even when it comes to something as seemingly mundane as the sun and the moon.

We're all very accustomed to there being twelve months in a year, but actually there are thirteen months - lunar months, that is. It takes approximately 28 days for the phases of the moon to cycle from dark (new) to light (full) and back again. Simple math (28 x 13 = 364) will tell us that thirteen lunar months can fit into a 365-day solar year.

A lunar month always begins with the dark (or new) moon - which is probably why we even call it the new moon. The origin of the name is fairly simply to deduce - all things begin in darkness. Whether it's a plant growing from a seed deep in the soil, a child developing in a womb, or the birth of a new day, each begins in darkness, just like the lunar month.

Beginnings are tiny things, almost unnoticeable by those who aren't looking for them. Imagine that we've gathered to watch a huge fireworks display. From the perspective of the waiting crowd, the display begins the moment that the first firework erupts across the sky. However, those of us on an occult path seek out the hidden secrets of the world. (Occult literally means "hidden" in case you're curious). For us, the fireworks display begins when the presenter extends his or her hand in the darkness and ignites the first fuse.

Likewise, the lunar month begins at its hidden (darkest) point. The full moon isn't the end of the cycle, but its mid-point, for each thing that grows in power (the waxing moon) will also fade (the waning moon). Every twenty-eight days the moon is born, reaches its fullness, and then fades into darkness. Every twenty-eight days we're reminded anew of the process of birth, life, death, and rebirth as the moon crosses our sky. The phases of the moon follow a regular progression. Starting with the darkness of the new moon, the moon waxes to full and then from full, wanes to new.

The traditional symbolism of the moon is pretty obvious given what we've discussed to this point:

The dark moon is when things begin anew.
The waxing moon is when the power grows.
The full moon is when the power is at its peak.
The waning moon is when the power fades.

Synchronizing the timing of a rite to a particular phase of the moon or connecting our ritual to the lunar cycle is a sure way of integrating this symbolism in our rite.

However, there are two more pieces of symbolism reflected in the moon that I find much more useful.

The first is the light of the moon itself. Realistically, the moon is just a big chunk of rock and dust. It doesn't create any light of its own. The light we see on the moon is the reflection of the sun on the moon's surface and the phases of the moon are from the Earth getting in the way and casting its shadow upon the moon.

With this in mind, I like to think of the phases of the moon as a door. During the new moon, the door is shut and the power behind it is locked away. When the moon is full, the door is wide open and the energy radiates unhindered. When the moon is waxing, the door is opening; when it's waning, the door is closing.

Imagine that you celebrate with a group of practitioners who have learned their entire path from nature. You've chosen one night to gather on which to raise energy together and interact as a group with the spirit world. That

chosen night is when the moon is full. Choosing to gather
when the power is most abundant quietly whispers a great
deal about the motivation and focus of your path and your
workings as a group. Choosing to gather when the "door"
to the mystical is wide open says something else altogether.
Both examples represent a valid gathering on the night of the
full moon, but perspective is a powerful thing. If symbolism
is the language of magick and symbolism is based primarily
on how deeply and strongly we connect with a concept, a
simple shift in how we see a concept can reap significant
magickal dividends.

The other piece of symbolism is what I like to refer to
as a "cosmic reminder."

Everywhere you look in life, there are cosmic
reminders. Think of them as little notes from the Divine that
help point the way on your path. Let's say, for instance, that
you're going through a tremendously challenging period
and you can't see the light at the end of the tunnel. You're
lost in the dark.

Much like the new moon.

From darkness, light is born. It's one of the stories that
the moon tells us. With its own cosmic reminder it whispers,
"Keep going. Keep looking. The light will come once more."
Likewise, when we find ourselves facing an obstacle that's
simply bigger than we can handle, we're reminded that all
things fade, like the full moon fading once more.

We are never truly alone on our paths. Each moment
is sacred; for pagans, especially once you learn where to look,
that statement isn't only true, but it becomes harder and
harder to overlook.

If you spent much time outdoors as a child, you may
have stumbled across a very simple concept that has been
lost to a chunk of the modern magickal community: while the
sun is associated with the day, the moon is not magickally
connected with the night.

I can't count the number of summer afternoons that
my friends and I would lay on the grass and stare up at the
sky, watching the moon cross the heavens in full daylight. A
typical sunny afternoon would find us off in the midst of grass
and trees, our bikes unceremoniously dumped somewhere
nearby. After hours of splashing through nearby streams,

having mock battles that transformed discarded sticks into epic swords and spears, we'd pause, stretch out on the earth to watch the clouds and talk about life, looking up to find Luna slowly crossing the blue sky.

One of the reasons many people connect the sun with the day and the moon with the night is the concept that each celestial object is the brightest object in their respective sky. The moon clearly dominates the night as the sun does the day. Our concept of "day" is measured from the rising of the sun in the east until it sets in the west. The moon does not have a similar role where night is concerned. While the sun is at the heart of the concept of "daytime", the moon isn't even always found in the night sky. Moonrise changes by approximately fifty minutes each day. This means that if the moon rose at midnight one day, approximately two weeks later it would rise at noon. While we may not realize it, the moon spends as much time in the daytime heavens as it does in the night sky.

To use the language of a shaman, "Day and night are gifts of the sun." We typically think of the rising of the sun as the beginning of the day and the setting of the sun as night. The symbolism associated with this language is the first challenge we have in understanding the power available to us.

Unraveling Illusion

When we say, "The rising sun," our minds are filled with an image of our nearest star rising from the horizon in the east and climbing into the sky. The subconscious thought here, regardless of what we know of science, is that the sun is moving across our sky. It's a very simple position to argue in support of as you can stand outside and actually watch this process with your own eyes.

However, the passage of the sun is an illusion, like looking in a mirror and believing there's another world in there as you can clearly see the reflection of your reality in the glass. A more accurate description of the process would be to say that the sun is (essentially) standing still and the Earth has rotated so that our side of the planet now faces the sun.

Imagine that you are standing at the outside edge of a merry-go-round with your back toward the center of the ride. Someone has drawn a line down the center of the park with the merry-go-round at the exact middle of the line. On one side of this line, the entire park has been painted white; the other side of the park has been painted black. As the merry-go-round slowly turns, the landscape in front of you will turn from white to black and back to white again in an endless cycle.

If we called the portion of the park that was painted white "day" and the black portion "night" this would be a much more accurate way of looking at the process we observe from our place here on Earth. What we refer to as "day" is simply when our portion of the Earth is bathed in the sun's light. "Night" is when we are in the Earth's shadow, cast by sunlight falling on the other side of our planet.

THE POWER OF THE SUN

For all practical purposes, the sun isn't moving. Our portion of the planet is rotating in and out of the sun's light. From this perspective, it's not the rising and setting of the sun that is so important, as the transition of the world around us from the black portion of the park to the white portion of the park and back again. It isn't simply the presence of the sun that empowers the moment, but the simple fact that there are transitions occurring as we move in and out of the sun's light.

Whenever we work magick, we're seeking to create change. One of the key components we can use in this process is the symbolism at sunrise or sunset, of the transformation of the landscape around us from day to night or from night to day. It's not the sun that is moving. At sunrise we are moving from a period of darkness into a period of light. At sunset, we are moving from a period of light into one of darkness. This is powerful symbolism that we can utilize in our rites.

Adding to this power is the symbolism of the sun itself. We see the sun from our vantage point (a nearly unfathomable distance from our star) as a powerful, life-giving, illuminating source. The sun, however, is an entire dictionary worth of symbolism. From the unrelenting heat of a drought to a calm daybreak after a fierce storm, from the sunburn of betrayal (literally referred to as "getting burned") to the warmth of a lover's caress, seen from different perspectives, the sun holds the symbolism of nearly every experience available to us as human beings.

The key to beginning to understand the power of using the sun in ritual work isn't its association with the day, but the sun's role on the level of our planet, our solar system, and our position in the galaxy.

A VERY BIG PLACE

Light travels at approximately 300,000 kilometers (seven times around the Earth) in one second. With this as our measuring stick, the moon is approximately 1.3 light seconds from Earth.

The sun, on the other hand, is approximately 500 light seconds from Earth – or almost 400 times farther from us than the moon. It takes light eight minutes to travel from the sun to the Earth and 1.3 seconds for sun's light to reflect off of the moon and reach our planet.

To put things in perspective, it's probably more useful to think of "working with the sun and the moon" as "working with our local star and our planet's satellite." The second designation paints the landscape before us with significantly more clarity.

CORE SYMBOLISM

At the level of basic ritual magick, the symbolism associated with the sun and the moon is very similar. The moon describes a particular pattern of journeying energy, from new to waxing to full to waning to new once more. In working with lunar energy, this symbolism represents an endless cycle of birth, life, death and rebirth. Likewise, this pattern is mirrored in the sun from sunrise to strengthening daylight to noon to fading daylight to sunset.

The key difference between the two is the power of transition. When the sun rises, it brings daylight with it. When it sets, it ushers in the night. While the moon both rises and sets, it doesn't transform the world from day to night in the same way that the sun alters the landscape.

And that's the key where lunar work begins to pull away from solar magick - the level of what it changes.

SOLITARY AND COMMUNAL

The greatest challenge before us is grasping the scale associated with working with the sun and the moon. When we look to the sky, both the sun and the moon are bright celestial bodies. One illuminates the day; one illuminates the night. In fact, depending on astronomical conditions, the moon can even appear substantially larger than the sun in our sky.

If we were to step in a spacecraft and leave the Earth, the moon would rapidly disappear from view, followed a short time later by the Earth. The Earth would appear as a bright star for a time, before fading into the background and completely disappearing from sight. Our sun, however, would remain too bright to look upon for a nearly unimaginable distance.

This concept is key to unlocking the symbolism associated with the sun and moon in deeper magick.

See, the moon belongs only to the Earth. It is merely our companion in the sky, sometimes there during the day, sometimes present during the night. Step even a short distance away (in astronomical terms) and the moon rapidly disappears on the larger scale. Literally disappears. It simply isn't part of the greater celestial landscape. The sun, however, remains a part of the heavens even when we move so far from Earth that we realize our sun is simply another star in the sky.

What we find here are two very different celestial bodies that represent similar processes on two completely different scales.

For instance, the moon speaks of the cycle of birth, life, death, and rebirth over the course of the twenty-eight day lunar month. The sun and the cycle of the seasons describe the same process as the lunar month, but take approximately 365 days to do so. The moon glows with reflected sunlight, gently illuminating the night; the sun illuminates the entire landscape, driving shadows before it.

THE SECRET

The key difference is something that most modern practitioners overlook - but the symbolism speaks volumes.

The sun is the source of the light.

The moon is a mirror.

The sun is the star at the center of our solar system. All life and light on our planet are directly related to this star and our entire solar system orbits around Sol.

The moon is a chunk of rock and dust which orbits the Earth in much the same way that the Earth orbits the sun. The moon doesn't create any light of its own, but simply reflects the light of the sun and the shadow of the Earth.

Sol, our sun, is the center of our solar system and each body that orbits around Sol (including the Earth) belongs to our star. All of the planets, comets, asteroids, and other bodies that orbit around Sol speak in some way to the sun's journey, mirroring our star's own path. In a similar manner, Luna, our moon, belongs to the Earth - and she mirrors that which our planet experiences.

For instance, the journey of the sun changes all of the natural world wherever that life is open to and connected to its energy. Snows melt, flowers blossom, plants bend toward the light – the change the sun brings stretches from horizon to horizon. Likewise, the journey of the moon changes all who are open to and connect to its energy - including the tides and those of us who look to Luna for inspiration and insight. The sun represents communal energy and transformation, symbolized by all it touches. Luna represents individual energy and transformation because it works its change on a much smaller scale when compared to the sun.

To put it in simple terms, if the moon was a benevolent sorceress, the sun would be her patron deity and the source of her power. Anyone can come to the sorceress in their time of need and receive aid directly from her. Her patron deity, while more distant and unapproachable, shines upon all, not working with an individual but on a scale so large it's difficult for us to comprehend.

This is the key component to consider when utilizing the power of the sun or moon in our rites. When we need to create personal transformation – a single step at a time – we work with the moon. Lunar energy allows us to create quick, defined change on a relatively short scale. When the transformation we seek is larger, long term, and has the potential to interact with many lives, we work with solar energy, simply because of the symbolism it represents. While the sun is a distant, all-powerful force, the moon is a mirror and a fellow traveler much like ourselves.

SUN MAGICK

Our modern calendar is a little off. Here in the West, the first day on our calendar is January 1st - a little more than a week after the start of the solar year (approximately December 21st).

What most of us lose sight of in our modern world is that it's not just "a year" - it's a journey of light.

You've probably noticed as you go through your year that the days are longer during the summer and shorter during the winter. While it may not be something that you've consciously thought about, you've probably noticed the journey of light just the same. In the summer months, this phenomena translates to something typically known as, "Stupid sun! It's Saturday and I'm trying to sleep in! Why are you up already?" or just as frequently as, "Mom! Why do we have to go to bed now? It's still light outside." During the winter months, our modern culture often describes this process as, "It's dark when I leave for work; it's dark when I leave work to go home."

Here in the northern hemisphere (and that's key), Winter Solstice, approximately December 21st, is the shortest day of the year. Another way to think of it is that it's the day a portion of your co-workers are most likely to complain about no longer seeing the sun because they're at work. If you were to measure the hours of sunlight against the hours of darkness, there are fewer hours of light on this day than any other.

Each day from Winter Solstice until Summer Solstice (approximately June 21st) the hours of sunlight grow in number. You guessed it - Summer Solstice has more hours of light than any day of the year. But it's more than that.

We're pretty disconnected from nature in our modern world, but imagine that you spend a great deal of time outdoors instead of at a computer. In today's world, if your Internet connection goes down, it's a pretty big deal. When your favorite social networking site goes offline, even for a few hours, it makes the news. Now imagine that you live in a world where you're unplugged from the machine and spend your days surrounded by trees, fresh air, and sunlight. Imagine how monumental it is in your world to watch the hours of sunlight fade, in some latitudes almost to nothing, and then slowly grow again once more. This journey happens every year without fail.

What's more is that as the sunlight fades, plants begin to die. Migratory animals disappear. The food sources that you embraced during the warmer months are scarce or gone altogether. How sacred would it be to observe a single day each year when you knew the hours of sunlight would begin to grow once more? How much power would a day hold when the dying sun would be reborn and grow in power and light, literally changing the landscape around you?

Pagans typically honor both of the solstices (the day when the hours of daylight begin to grow and the day when they begin to fade), as well as a handful of other days related to the journey of the sun, as holy days. These days are often referred to as Sabbats but other names, such as the Asatru (Norse paganism) term *blot*, are also used.

What is often challenging for us to relate to in our modern world is that a year isn't simply a string of days and a turning of pages on a calendar. A solar year is a journey of light and life, where both are born, grow, mature, age and die. This cycle is repeated endlessly, beginning anew with each solar year (at the Winter Solstice) and turning full circle in what many of us refer to as the Wheel of the Year until it ends at the same place the following year. This journey is rich with symbolism, energy and magick that can be relied upon, mirrored, and integrated into our rites.

Because our planet is tilted on its axis, the northern and southern hemispheres experience the seasons at opposite times. When it's winter in the United Kingdom, it's summer in Australia. When the United States is experiencing spring, New Zealand is embracing fall. It's an excellent reminder that our paths are very diverse and even when you're embracing Winter Solstice and themes of snow and ice, chances are you're connected to another pagan who is spending their free time in a swimsuit at the beach.

MOON MAGICK

The new moon and full moons are very magickal times. Generally speaking, most lunar magick is worked with the waxing or waning moons, simply because much of the spellwork we do requires something to be created or supported (waxing) or banished or grounded (waning). The easiest way to consider these days is to think of the journey of the sun. Days of the quarter moons are similar to the spring and autumnal equinoxes. When we look at the moon, the light and darkness are equal just as the hours of sunlight are equal on the equinoxes that happen each spring and fall. The full and new moons are similar to the summer and winter solstices. We simply don't think of the pattern of lunar energy this way because the phases of the moon are a cycle; when observing the sun, we can see that its journey "stops" and reverses course on the solstices.

Various magickal groups gather on the nights of the full and new moons for this reason. They're magickal days when the moonlight is at its highest or lowest points. We've considered that the moon symbolizes singular energy (while the sun symbolizes communal energy) and we gather communally on these nights as the moon's light has reached one of two extremes. It's much more common for a pagan group (a coven or circle, for example) to gather on the full moon than it is for them to gather on the new moon. Symbolically, the moon has "gathered" all of its light on the full moon, so we gather together as a group. The rest of the lunar month we do solitary work by the moonlight as the moon itself is keyed to singular (or solitary) energy.

Celebrations, healing work, blessings - anything that could be expressed in a joyful exclamation is perfect to do on the full moon as it is the epitome of light. Likewise, shadow work (working with the "darker" aspects of ourselves), banishing, and anything that could be whispered or hidden is the domain of the dark (or new) moon.

I've heard it argued countless times that the new moon is the time of beginnings. And I agree with this completely and even teach it myself, especially if you work your rite immediately after the moon has moved from "waning to new" and is solidly in the "waxing to full." It's important to do "beginnings" work when the energy is raising, not when it's fading. (Traditionally speaking, any rite can be worked within three days of the actual astronomical event, but there are times - such as with the new moon - when you want to be careful of what the energy is doing when you work your ritual.)

The moon is the Earth's closest celestial neighbor and this closeness makes Luna the perfect choice to empower us for challenging portions of our path. When we find ourselves working magick to help us confront a challenge, connecting that rite to the lunar cycle will bring help in a more immediate form (a door opening, a friend coming with an answer, etc.) while working with the sun will shift things on a more Universal level. (For instance, while the situation itself may not work out, it will position you for the next step of your path - which in the "bigger scheme of things" is the intended outcome). It's also this symbolism that makes the moon a poor choice, in my opinion, to use in a ritual designed to gain insight unless you're only intending to see the immediate energetic landscape. The moon is simply reflected sunlight and as such its perspective is very limited. Connecting such work to the sun will offer a farther reaching answer. You will, however, need to either understand the situation at hand or be strongly drawn to one result of the other, as tying your rite to either the sun or the moon can make the other vibrational response (immediate or universal) harder for you to see.

We also work with the moon when we want either a) quick results, b) less powerful results (a nudge, rather than a shove) or c) both. The sun is exactly the opposite - workings tied to the sun tend to unfold slowly and are much more powerful. There are exceptions to this, but they require multi-part rites to fully connect to the appropriate energy and move beyond the obvious flow.

One of my favorite bits of symbolism associated with the moon is also one of the most simple. If the sun represents collective energy, then it also means that it's a distant presence (in both real and magickal terms). Powerful? Absolutely. Distant? Definitely, especially considering that the sun is so far away that it takes sunlight eight minutes to reach our planet. The moon, however, is not on the same scale of power as the sun and is much closer than our local star. I was working with a young student once and explaining this aspect of the sun and moon to them, which they interpreted like this:

"The sun is like the President. They have a lot of power, but if you called them on the phone they probably wouldn't help you right away - they're running a whole country and have other things to do first. The moon is like your best friend. If you called them and asked for help, they'd be there as quickly as possible. They may not be able to bring the army with them, but they'd know what to say to make it better and you could play together."

Out of the mouths of babes. I can't think of a better way to explain it myself.

CHAPTER FOURTEEN

PHYSICAL MAGICK

It's commonly understood in mystical circles that "All is One," but for argument's sake, let's create an artificial division of reality. In this reality we have three levels: Tangible, Conceptual, and Ethereal. Tangible is defined as anything we can touch. Conceptual includes everything we can think or imagine. Those things which lay beyond our ability to touch or conceptualize fall into the realm of the Ethereal.

In this reality we've created, we want to add the concept of Magick. Magick, in our artificially created world, is simply the process of altering reality through non-Tangible means.

Countless Seekers (those who are drawn to explore the mysteries of our artificial world) choose Magick as their tool to unravel the weave of reality. One of the Seekers comes up with the idea that seems obvious to us: in order to alter Tangible reality through non-Tangible means requires interacting with either the Conceptual or Ethereal.

Still with me?

Because we have a very similar concept in our world.

Most of the magick that we practice on our paths is deeply connected to what we'd refer to as the Tangible in our artificial reality. For instance, casting a circle often includes the creation of sacred (yet physical) space. Those of us who call Elements are bringing in Conceptual representatives of the Tangible in our own world – in this case Air, Fire, Water and Earth.

There's both a problem with this approach and a reason we utilize it.

The challenge is that magick is highly symbolic. We may not realize it, but every time we draw a circle, call an Element, or light a candle, we're not only utilizing the symbolism and energy represented in that object, but we're also further connecting ourselves to the physical realm with each step further into the ritual. It's an interesting dilemma. Calling Air into our Circle, for instance, raises the available energy but simultaneously connects us with an Element that is intimately part of the physical realm. Add Fire to the mix, the energy raises farther and our Circle is further anchored.

Here's an easier way to describe the situation: To raise energy, we rely on the symbolism of physical concepts (the Elements, lighting candles, defining sacred space, etc.) in order to work magick. It's similar to a movie wizard putting a magical potion into an alcoholic beverage – the imbiber not only gains the effect of the potion, but grows more intoxicated at the same time.

The juxtaposition of energy and the physical world explains much of the phenomena we observe during ritual magick. Candles often burn much slower or faster than they should and time flows at a unpredictable rate. Ritual magick works simply because we've raised so much energy. However, our circle becomes a bubble (more on that in a moment) in which we bend the flow of reality. This combination stretches the weave so that it's easy to package our intent and push it through the veil. This is why we often describe being in Circle as "Being between the worlds." (This entire concept is illusionary when seen from the perspective of deeper magickal work but it gets across the point I'm trying to convey).

The other half of the equation is that we've built ourselves a protective bubble in which to work. Some traditions actually intend for the circle to function in this manner. In fact, the long version of Wiccan Rede states, "[cast or tread] the Circle thrice about to keep unwelcome spirits out." Using a circle as a protective boundary is so effective that folklore is saturated with people doing just that. From a symbolic perspective, creating a circle (regardless of whether it's drawn or cast), separates that space from the world around it. Yes, that allows us to raise a tremendous amount of mystical energy within its boundary, but it also forms a protective bubble that is grounded in physical reality. Why? Because the best protection against spiritual energies is to ground them in physical reality.

That seems incredibly counter-intuitive approach to mystical workings, but ritual magick is very much that way.

The easiest way for us to understand this concept is to use a common light bulb as a rough example. Current flows into it, it generates light and heat, and the glass casing surrounding the filament both allows it to illuminate a room while keeping the room from touching the filament. In this example, the light bulb is connected to two worlds (electricity and the room beyond the bulb) simultaneously. While it can take the energy it's summoning (from the light socket the bulb is screwed into) and illuminate the room, it is still protected from the room by its casing. From an energetic perspective, it's easiest to understand a circle in this way if we consider that the boundary of our circle is the light bulb's casing, the electricity is the energy we raise, the light our intent, and the room the bulb illuminates (changing from dark to light) is the greater flow of reality.

Ritual magick is effective, but it approaches the task of altering reality from a position rooted in the physical. That doesn't mean – and let me make this absolutely clear – that ritual magick is not an effective approach to magick. It absolutely is effective and I rely on it a great deal in my own practice. What it does do is insinuate that there are other approaches to magick that wait to be explored further down the path. With this idea in mind, there is one key reason why we utilize ritual magick, a reason that we may not have ever stopped to consider.

Ritual magick teaches us to embrace symbolism, not simply how to use it in our rites, but it lays the pathways for us to begin to think symbolically. In other words, ritual magick and its heavy reliance on symbolism form the key that opens the next door on our path.

When we begin to embrace symbolism, we step away from the physical nature of that object. For instance, if I look over to one of my favorite books sitting on the bookshelf, I don't think of it as being a collection of paper and ink. I don't even consider the publishing process that went into its creation. When I look at the book, my mind is filled with a kaleidoscope of images and stories that the book holds. It's no longer a book that I see, but a symbol of the journey of knowledge held within its pages.

Symbolism is the next step in our journey, but it's limiting in its own right simply because we create it to be so. The book I'm looking at is flanked by two other books. When I look at each, the stories they contain appear in my mind's eye in turn. I don't know about you, but each book that I read is also "narrated" by a different voice. In a way, books are symbolic of the author and the story that author tells.

However, each book is only one story. The story that the book holds is told only the author who penned the tale. I don't open a book on the Tao and find stories of the myths and legends of Norway.

But I could.

Conceptual magick is the practice of letting go of the physical to fully embrace the symbolism. This removes us another step farther from the tangible world and a step closer to the spiritual realm. The most common example of conceptual magick is a guided meditation or journeying. In this process we leave the physical behind to embrace a world of symbolism that is free of constraints.

What may be surprising is that we're almost as familiar with this world as we are with the physical world around us. Each of us visits this conceptual, symbol-based world in our dreams.

There's a reason why dreams are so critical to shamanic work. It's in the same realm our minds visit in our dreams that the next level of magick takes place. The interesting thing is what happens when we begin to use this world.

We have conceptual space already in place that we frequently use without giving it a second thought. It's how we dream. Our consciousness needs a path to follow to shift into the dreamscape and we can follow this same path in our own magickal work. Doing magick in the conceptual realm is very different than the ritual work we do in the tangible world. A bit earlier we considered the thought that, to put it simply, yes, we can actually move to a "spiritual plane" and work our magick there.

Conceptual magick is worked entirely on a non-physical plane. We literally pursue the same paths that we use in shamanic journeying, reach a place of power (a symbolic sacred site), and work our magick in that place without moving a muscle in the physical world. With each step into the realm of symbolism (something taught by ritual magick) you'll find that you gain a greater ability to manifest any reality you choose in, for lack of better vocabulary, the meditative part of your mind. This is your reality, a world completely yours to weave, bend, and shape. Here you will find teachers, knowledge, and the information that you need to continue deeper into the mysteries.

Remember, symbolism is the language of magick. In a completely symbolic realm, you are standing in the midst of magick. There is no need to raise energy and no need to construct a circle to separate, anchor, or protect you. Here, a book doesn't simply hold an author's story; it holds all the stories written by all the authors in all the realities that ever were or have yet to be. Here you don't call the Elements. They come to you. They are you. Your only limitations are those you place on yourself.

Like ritual magick, conceptual magick both anchors and protects itself. Both anchor and circle come in the form of your own ego. At this point of the journey, we are still attached to the idea that we are separate from the greater weave of reality. The change we weave doesn't simply manifest, it is cast from your mind. It is still magick of your choosing and your working. Our natural walls, defenses, and need for control insulate and protect us in the same manner that physical elements and a cast circle do in ritual magick.

Where ritual magick taught us symbolism as a tool to progress in our craft, conceptual magick teaches us to surrender our need to define ourselves to move even farther down the path. We drop walls, filters, and daily become more truly our higher or core self. As you begin to clearly see the Divine within you in the reflection of your core self, you also see the Divine in others. This understanding creates a resonance and the understanding that our limitations are truly illusionary. We begin to see that we aren't simply working magick; we are magick. If all things are truly One then, when we unlock this next door, there are no more limitations.

At this point of the journey, we can use the term ethereal magick in order to understand the shift, but we no longer seek to control the process. Labels are no longer necessary. The surrendering of ego and fear and the opening to love and harmony has brought us to a place of balance and harmony. Magick still happens when we will it, but it is accomplished with a thought, a word, or a simple gesture. Much of the time, however, magick simply happens in the world around us and we respond to it just as the weave of reality responds to us.

My path continually nudges into this territory, but I am neither experienced enough nor arrogant enough to pretend that I fully understand more than a fraction of what I've experienced. As you grow closer to this point, magick begins to seep into every part of your world. Much of it is a subtle saturation that comes from being open to the oneness of reality. However, there are simply moments where reality shifts beyond the mundane into something that is truly magickal. It's not just that you can reach out to the fabric of reality, but that the fabric of reality can reach out to you. Instead of seeking teachers, they come to us. The spirit world has a tendency to step into our world when we're open to it doing so.

There are two things that I feel are important to understand in this process.

The first is that it's a journey. In it we not only learn deeper forms of magick but we transform ourselves and the way we see all of reality.

Letting go of our fear, we begin to explore ritual magick. Ritual magick is effective, but it approaches the task of altering reality from a position rooted in the physical. It teaches us to embrace symbolism, which is the "protective circle" used in conceptual magick.

With a deep understanding of magick and symbolism, we embrace conceptual magick. A step closer to interacting with the flow of reality, conceptual magick teaches us the surrender of self and the embrace of oneness. The concept of self is the "protective circle" used in conceptual magick, and when we release it, we can fully embrace the concept of oneness.

With our walls dropped, we can begin to embrace ethereal magick which is worked from within the flow of reality. It teaches us love for all manifestation which is the work of the Divine.

The second concept is that this is not a linear journey with a beginning and a destination. It is a spiral path that turns ever upward. Even after we've stepped into higher forms of magick, we will return to ritual magick from time to time and learn additional concepts and insights with our new perspective. Imagine, for example, someone who has gained a tremendous amount of skill in conceptual magick applying that skill to ritual magick working.

Likewise, with each turn of the path, we see more, learn more, and grow more. These forms of magick are not labels, levels, or badges of honor. Being skilled in conceptual magick does not make you a better person or a better practitioner than someone who only embraces ritual magick. Everything is One and the forms of magick are nothing more than tools that we have in our spiritual tool box.

For instance, imagine that we could go back in time and that all of us were part of the same tribe. With food scarce, we decide that we would hunt for deer and that we would use magick to ensure the success of the hunt.

Embracing ritual magick, we would put on skins and antlers and dance around the fire, summoning the spirit of the deer to us. The next day we would hunt and find a deer grazing in a meadow.

Embracing conceptual magick, we would go deep into trance and work our magick there. The next day we would hunt and the deer would unexpectedly walk up to us.

Embracing ethereal magick, we open to the Universe, and the next day an unknown hunter comes into our camp and offers us the deer he's slain as a gift.

If one path was better than another, we could measure it in the success of the hunt. Which form of magick brought us deer to eat? All of them resulted in our tribe being fed. Each, however, had a result that was a mirror of the tools used in that form of magick. Ritual magick is rooted in the physical - so we simply conducted a physical hunt and had success doing so. Conceptual magick begins to release boundaries and the deer unexpectedly walked up to our hunting party. Ethereal magick embraces the oneness of all and the weave of reality simply presented us the food we'd requested.

This is merely a glimpse of the path ahead; something to get you thinking about your own magickal workings and where they're taking you. If that wasn't enough to get you thinking, keep this in mind: If all truly is One, then every division – time, incarnation, whatever you can imagine – is also an illusion. While we may not have the skills, perspective, and growth necessary to step beyond each and every boundary, it gives us an idea of the landscape we have to explore.

Coming Soon

A Year and a Day: A Hands-On Experiential Training Guide in Modern Magick

BIOGRAPHY

Jeffrey Pierce is a best-selling novelist, exhibited photographer, indie filmmaker, and traditionally trained shaman. On March 21, 1987, he embarked on a quest to see beyond the veil of religion and find the divine for himself. The quest led through nearly every major religion on Earth and countless regional indigenous systems of belief. He taught classes and workshops, preached in churches, led covens, and studied under an amazing line of teachers including a Native American shaman and an old Roma crone.

He began teaching spirituality in 1992 and founded Old Ways in March 1997. Unlike many spiritual teachers, Jeffrey is extremely reluctant to accept payment for instruction, which is one of the key reasons why Old Ways is offered completely free of charge. To maintain his ethical standards where his role as a spiritual teacher is concerned, you'll often find him sharing excerpts from upcoming books via Old Ways and the site's associated Facebook group months in advance of the book's publication.

In addition to the work he does with Old Ways, Jeffrey is a husband and father, relishing the time that he spends with his family. An avid backpacker and outdoorsman, he spends a great deal of time in the mountains, forests, and along the beaches in his native Pacific Northwest. To unwind, he prefers playing online games with his friends or dabbling in numerous artistic mediums.

In addition to fiction and non-fiction writing projects, Jeffrey is hard at work on the upcoming documentary series, "Sacred Nature."

Old Ways was established by Jeffrey Pierce on March 21, 1997 to provide instruction and insight to seekers on a path of mystical spirituality. Articles, daily lessons, and original informational and instructional videos are all offered completely free of charge.

WWW.OLDWAYS.COM

You can contact Jeffrey Pierce at

CONNECT@OLDWAYS.COM

CPSIA information can be obtained at www.ICGtesting.com
Printed in the USA
LVOW13s2202090813

347195LV00020B/560/P

9 780615 785547